Tango
Lessons / for Life

A perspective on healing and life as seen
through the eyes of a dancing doctor

Jeannette Potts, M.D.

Cleveland Clinic Press

Cleveland, Ohio

Tango: Lessons for Life

A perspective on healing and life as seen through the eyes of a dancing doctor

Cleveland Clinic Press
All rights reserved
Copyright © 2007 Cleveland Clinic

Contact:
Cleveland Clinic Press
9500 Euclid Avenue NA32
Cleveland, Ohio 44195
216-445-5547
delongk@ccf.org
www.clevelandclinicpress.org

This book is not intended to replace personal medical care and supervision; there is no substitute for the information and experience that your doctor can provide.

The patient names and cases used in this book are composites drawn from several sources.

Library of Congress Cataloging-in-Publication Data
Potts, Jeannette M.
Tango: Lessons for Life: A perspective on healing and life as seen through the eyes of a dancing doctor / Jeannette Potts.
p. cm.
Includes index.
ISBN 978-1-59624-040-7 (alk. paper)
1. Potts, Jeannette M.   2. Urologists--Ohio--Cleveland--Biography.
3. Tango (Dance)   4. Medicine--Philosophy.   I. Title.
RC870.92.P68A3 2007   616.60092--dc22
[B]
2007020765

Cover and book design: Meredith Pangrace
Cover photo: Eric Mull
Interior photos: Steve Travarca, Cleveland Clinic Center for Medical Art and Photography

Dedication

This book is dedicated to my Abuelita ("Grandma"), Lida Saul. She's 88 years old and lives in Mexico City.

A consistent source of gifts since my childhood, she's a nostalgic singer, a sensuous poet, a talented cook, a music aficionado, an ardent fan of bullfighting, and, most important, a passionate dancer.

Acknowledgments

I would like to thank the following people.

Benjamin Gleisser, a gifted author who thoughtfully organized and burnished my story. (His sensibilities are like those of a good *tanguero*.)

Rick Ramos (somarkcir@hotmail.com), my very first tango teacher, who was successful in "taming the shrew" on the dance floor.

"El Sueco," who said in 2002, "This would make a nice book …"

Jorge Niedas of 21 Tango (www.21tango.com). After dancing in Cleveland, New York, Chicago, San Francisco, Montreal, Buenos Aires, and Mexico City, I can say that I've never had another teacher/partner with such tremendous agility, strength, and aesthetics. (He lifted me up upon one of his feet and led me into the most provocative of *ganchos* and most elegant of *colgadas*!) Ironically, he's the most modest teacher and performer I've ever met. (Jorge is my partner in the photos that appear on pages 101 through 104.)

David Palmer, my elegant, generous, and reliable tango partner, who, despite his busy work schedule, joined me at TV stations, photo shoots, and seminars of all kinds to perform with Dr. Tango.

My sister, Elaine Kuether, the enthusiastic board member of the Dr. Tango enterprise – the one who said "go for it!" as she has done so many times before. Thoughtful and generous, she's the ideal sister and all-essential aunt for my children.

Nicki Artese of Artese Communications, marketing consultant for Dr. Tango. I'm blessed to work with a person of such integrity. Her generosity, work ethic, and wit are immeasurable. Her positive attitude when confronted with challenges is inspiring.

Bradley, my marvelous son and cautious business advisor, who has exhibited patience and maturity beyond his years. And Ellen, my beautiful daughter and artistic director, who has enthusiastically embraced the concept of "tango as healer." Their father and I are very proud of them, and we agree that if we were teenagers at this moment, Bradley and Ellen would be our best friends.

Table of Contents

continued on next page

Table of Contents (continued)

Introduction

*"Sabes tu lo que yo haria en esos momentos de indignacion?
Te arrancaria el Corazon ... para comermelo a besos!"*

*("Do you know what I would do in those moments of indignation?
I would rip out your heart ... so that I may devour it with my
kisses!")*

Confronting and surviving life's challenges joyously requires
a dance. And inevitably this dance of life leads people to
scuff their elegant shoes and stub those delicate toes. Dance
is a life-affirming challenge, and no one who is preoccupied
with keeping the luster on his shoes will ever feel the
courage to move forward.

Remember the movie *Shall We Dance?* Searching for
happiness, the protagonist discovers through dance that
joy and wholeness come from within, and when he finds
peace within himself, he discovers in his marriage, work, and
family the love he thought he had lost.

One needn't be a dancer to recognize the power of an
embrace or realize the sweetness of surrender to our loves
and passions. This book is a reminder for many of us who

have become too busy to enjoy the melodies and pauses in the music of our lives. The roots of the dance are the sounds we hear within our heartbeats.

As a physician who takes care of men with urological conditions, particularly those which cause pain and disability, I am frequently reminded of the importance of quality of life. How sad it is that too many people seem to take life for granted.

Knowing that I wanted to help my patients take better care of themselves, I asked myself what I could do to improve their outlook on life as well as their lives. Fortunately, I discovered Argentinian tango.

Tango is a musical genre that began in the late 1800s. Its roots stretch vast distances, as it was derived from African rhythms, European traditions, and finally hybridization in the ghettos of Buenos Aires and Montevideo. The dance is said to have begun in brothels as a means of showing off to perspective lovers or perhaps as an anticipatory prelude to sexual frolic. Outside the brothels, it belonged only to the lower social classes. To this day, some aristocratic Latin Americans turn up their noses at this dance. Unfortunately, they miss out on the universal passions and wholesome sensuality that are celebrated in the dance and its songs.

Tango captivated me. I was mesmerized by the nonverbal communication that occurs between man and woman on the dance floor, and realized that such effort could be applied to the rigors of daily life. Soon, "dance" became the verb of choice in my vocabulary. I danced with my children. I danced with co-workers. I danced with patients. I surrendered to their lead and ultimately derived courage and peace from doing so.

I came to believe that beyond its erotic mystique, tango's fusion of physics, artistry, and passion provocatively illustrates the dialogue of our daily lives. It breathes new strength and meaning into such words as cooperation, receptiveness, surrendering, and yielding.

As tango became more important to me, I felt at first that I was moving abruptly in and out of two disparate worlds, one being medicine and the other a world of music and art. But now I dance gracefully between the pragmatic and the sublime environments that define my existence. This realization has compelled me to share these metaphors in *Tango: Lessons for Life*.

My life in words

I've enjoyed writing short stories and poetry since I was a teenager and resumed writing regularly after my divorce. I also began taking tango lessons, reacquainting myself with my passion for dance. As these two passions of mine overlapped, I began to write more in my journal about the new dance moves I was learning. At first, I thought I was taking notes so as not to forget the steps required to accomplish a move successfully. But these technical notes began to include other insights I picked up during practice. Dance practice became my meditation, and my dance studio became my sacred space.

I ruminated over what it was in men's personalities that would allow mischievous interleading. I reflected over the complexities of embellishments and the balance between self-confidence and self-obsession. I wondered about the patterns that entrap us within the context of familiarity or of our biased and destructive expectations. I began to realize that my personal shortcomings could be readily identified on the dance floor, especially when I was brave enough to explore the whys and hows of a successful or failed maneuver. I began applying the physics of a dance move to the dynamics of interpersonal relationships, to work, and to home life. Even now, I remain challenged by the first rule of tango: *Do not anticipate* (particularly, I found, when it comes to child-rearing).

As my observations became more astute, my writing became more fluent. Since I am completely captivated by anything sensuous or erotic, it seems obvious in retrospect that a dance like tango would have spoken to me so eloquently.

My journal is the basis for this book. I share it now, hoping that it validates, informs, and brings laughter to those who read it. On a less altruistic note, I hope that many people will identify with the issues revealed in these pages, so that I won't feel like the only neurotic romantic, the only incompetent mother, or the only imperfect physician on the planet!

I hope you enjoy *Tango: Lessons for Life*.

Now … shall we dance?

More information about Dr. Potts, her workshops, and the Argentine tango is available at www.doctortango.net.

Chapter 1

The Embrace

Some people see life as a series of beginnings. Others experience reality as the challenge to meet one goal after another. Certainly, life is full of challenges and new beginnings, but I choose to live it as a series of dances – one dance giving way to the next and the next and the next …

We encounter people, change partners, find new partners. Sometimes we dance alone. Sometimes, we're surprised when a former partner walks back onto the dance floor, offers us a smile and a hand, and we dance together again as if the music we once heard together had never stopped.

Who are our dance partners? Look around you. We dance with those we grew up with, the people we work with, the people we live with. Our friends and lovers. Our teachers and children. The upstairs neighbor who plays his music too loudly. The shy supermarket cashier who blushes as she takes our money and looks away, smiling to herself, feeling glad to be alive, and realizing that the parade of shoppers eager to get through her line represents a wonderful chance to beam at so many potential new acquaintances.

This is why we keep on dancing. I believe nothing is more important than the dance. And like this worthy cashier, I, too, am looking forward to meeting many new friends.

Thank you for holding this book. Shall we begin?

First steps

Just as all beginnings contain the elements of mystery, arousal, and preparation, the initial physical act of tango is very exciting. And, sometimes it even causes a bit of fear. (Remember your first day on the new job? You wondered whether you could meet everyone's expectations and hoped your co-workers would like you. I'll bet that as soon as your confidence kicked in, you got over that initial hesitation pretty quickly.)

In terms of tango, the music signals our beginning. My partner approaches me and his posture invites me to join him, but as the woman, I will define the embrace. Tango etiquette lets me dictate whether our dance will feature a close or distant embrace, and my body language tells him how he's going to lead. He then cradles me in a loving manner, and from there, the posture is refined.

Let me define cradling, in terms of dance. If you were to hold a baby in a loving fashion, you'd hold her evenly, horizontally, in front of your chest. Similarly, the woman slides into the circle of embrace, which allows her arms to be cradled in similar fashion. From there, her partner's arms continue to wrap around her further, until her arm is above his shoulder or on his shoulder blade, and her forearm is cradled on top of his upper arm.

Sometimes the dancers are touching; however, as I said, the woman's comfort level dictates how close the dancers will be.

Even though the music has already started, the male dancer waits until the woman is settled. Believe it or not, people don't automatically begin moving with the first measure – they can start whenever they want to. In fact, this "delayed movement" is most appropriate for a couple's first dance, since at that point they don't know each other very well.

When the embrace becomes restrictive

The embrace is done lovingly, with no smothering or cramping. It needs to be done this way because if, for instance, later in the dance I am pivoting and my partner is holding me very closely, there is little room for me to maneuver. If he's controlling me too closely but expects me to execute a daring move with my leg when there isn't enough space for me to move, I'll feel stifled and restricted, as if he's forcing me to do something against my will. That can be very frustrating. Not only that, but there's physical discomfort as well. When I'm held too tightly, it hurts my back.

Think of this metaphorically. Think of some of the people you know who complain that they're being "held down" or "held back" on the job or in a personal relationship. Isn't it interesting how these people also often complain of back problems? It's as if these people are carrying too great a load; perhaps one partner is trying to carry the weight of two. Or a manager who's afraid of delegating authority feels as if she's "carrying the weight" of the whole department. If those people were able to share their loads – if they knew how to practice give-and-take with their partners – how much easier and more enjoyable their dance through life would be!

Believe me, it's wonderful when the space between partners is fluid. When I'm dancing, we can start out in a close embrace, so when the music begins to crescendo and I want to do more *fantasia* (a really big move), the circle between my partner and me just opens up. Our arms float apart. We're so connected, our movements become intuitive. There's a lot of sharing and my back is never bent unnaturally, so I don't feel any strain on my limbs. Our dancing is so natural that the only way I can describe it is to say that it just happens.

Life lesson: The power of the embrace

Just as the woman defines the boundaries in the dance, she also has the power to define boundaries in all of life's relationships. Yes, ladies, you're the ones who dictate the distance your comfort level requires. For many women, the discovery that they have the power to define the embrace is quite illuminating.

When some women realize that they had this power all along but hadn't thought to use it before, they become sad or angry. They look back over the years and feel as if they've been cheated. They regret that they haven't exercised this power and want to make up for lost time in a hurry. Don't fall into this trap. After all, anger and regret only lead to more anger and regret.

And if you're dancing with someone – a boss, lover, friend (of either sex), or someone else – who doesn't respect your power, stop dancing with that partner immediately. We should be careful not to end a dance or *tanda* – a set of dances – prematurely, for it's in dancing with others that we reveal valuable things to one another. But if we allow ourselves to be repeatedly squeezed, restricted, or stepped on, no matter how hard we try to redefine or adjust the embrace, we simply become accomplices to an ugly dance with unworthy partners.

Your power to set the rules should be respected. Being strong and assertive is a really wonderful thing. In fact, it actually enhances the dance and makes it more enjoyable. Why? Because in that situation, there exists mutual respect and trust, obviating the need for either rigid restraint or heavy clinginess.

Knowing a person's comfort level is important in every setting. Consider the workplace. If you don't know the people you're working with or their talents and strengths, you're not going to put them in the right position. For example, people who are very creative are often criticized by their left-brained counterparts as being "space cadets," while those freethinkers belittle the belittlers by putting their noses in the air and saying, "Oh, you're just a bunch of pencil-pushers."

It's the manager's job to match each worker with the right position, so that no one fails. A good leader also has to give his or her employees the chance to evolve. I think of the recent business metaphor "Right bus, right seat" – and translate it to "Right music, right shoes." Being a leader is quite a responsibility.

Unfortunately, some management and leadership positions are nothing more than inflated titles with higher pay. The privilege isn't balanced by the duty to care for and guide others. In tango, we readily recognize the coercive, entitled leadership style of the presumptuous man. And we come to feel deep respect for the man who humbly learns about those he will lead. He recognizes the importance of leading according to not only his own capabilities, but to those of his partner. And that starts with the embrace.

The embrace as a vulnerable gesture

As are all beginnings, the embrace is a very intimate position. No matter how far apart you are from the other person, there will always be hesitancy about moving forward. But it's necessary, if you want to take that first step. Don't let the music pass you by!

Allowing someone to come into your space is a courageous act. You're being fearless by recognizing your vulnerability and acting anyway. Go ahead, embrace a new person and allow him or her into your life. Just remember, you have the strength and power to define and dictate what the foundation of your new relationship will be. And, ultimately, there will be people whose comfort level lets you feel instantly able to dance heart-to-heart and cheek-to-cheek.

It also takes a lot of courage to express yourself. I'll talk more about this in other chapters, but first let me share a memory with you.

These are my first recollections of dancing. I was 3 years old, dancing by myself. I had tied all my mother's babushkas and silk scarves to my little bathing suit, and as I spun around and around in a circle, I felt those small banners of fabric swishing all over me. I might have done that because I was emulating some scene from a movie; perhaps I was pretending I was a belly dancer or Cleopatra. There was a ladder in the room because workers had been putting light fixtures up, and I danced around that ladder as if it were a stairway to heaven.

Because I wasn't self-conscious, I was totally lost in that very sensuous moment. I felt no fear – only pure joy. I remember looking down at myself, watching myself swirl like a top as all the stripes of color flowed out around me. Years later, after hundreds of lessons, I came to understand that when I danced, I was creating a sculpture that was never stationary. Being a dancer is like existing in four dimensions – the usual three dimensions that you experience when you look at an artistic object, plus a fourth type of knowing, whereby you also appreciate *being* the object. You can appreciate yourself from within, knowing that you're making this wonderful three-dimensional form.

This is why I love to dance. Even better, I love sharing my dance with others. When you dance, you're inviting someone to embrace and share your joy, and you share your confidence with that person. I say "confidence" because you know you possess the ability to create your dance, and now you're going to merge it with another person's perception of what the dance is. This is what the Argentines call "The Four-Legged Animal." You and your partner become one being with four legs.

Zen tango

It was said by the late beloved tango teacher known as Gavito, "The leader takes the follower into himself … as if she is his own back rib." I appreciate the power of this statement, as it describes the essence of the tango embrace. With confidence, passion, and purpose, the leader envelops the partner in his arms.

The embrace is a demonstration of our willingness to love, to explore, and to live. It is powerful because it contains both our vulnerability and our courage. For me, tango is like a religious ritual or spiritual journey. I believe the dance is a testament to faith through surrender, which can be easily translated to both the wonder and fragility of our lives. It's also a testament to the resilience we can show even in the most challenging circumstances.

Several years ago, I went to *Milonga*, in New York City. Most of us *tangueros* found seats along the sides of the dance studio. We removed our street shoes and pulled our special leather-soled shoes from our tango bags. This is a typical preparatory activity at all dance halls or studios, for we don't practice or dance without our special shoes. Both men and women performed the same ritual, whether tying laces or fastening tiny straps and buckles.

This simple act provided a point of transformation. It reminded me of martial-arts classes, when one enters a *dojo* and bows. Bowing is certainly a gesture of respect and reverence. However, we're also taught to perform the bow conscientiously and methodically, in order to change the focus of the mind. As an Aikido instructor explained to me many years ago, the bow symbolizes not only respect, but also the shedding of the outside world, which includes the mind's worries and distractions. We were supposed to be wholly present to the class and to ourselves. Practiced consistently, this simple exercise made me feel transported and peaceful. But now, instead of at the *dojo*, I can obtain such serenity on any smooth floor surface, especially wooden parquet.

After we adjusted our shoes, we listened to the music. Two tangos are never danced the same way, even if the song is repeated. Some of the dances can be quite melancholy. The lament in the lyrics of a tango *cancion* and the sorrowful melodies express a familiar sadness or sense of loss. Our culture has trained us to avoid such emotions, even when they apply to us in a personal way. But it almost seems as though we *tangueros* yearn for such heartfelt emotions. Perhaps we seek the physical embrace itself, so soothing and therapeutic. Or perhaps tango provides the sanctuary we may have been looking for at a subconscious level. We allow the melancholy to envelop us. For us, it's as much a part of our lives as the gaiety of the playful *milongas*. We embrace the melancholy as we do the joy. Both are equally valuable, significant, and beautiful. Both are part of life. Society would have us dodge unpleasantness, yet the unpleasant things are what make us grow. There is no hiding – no waiting for mirages of solace.

This dance with melancholy, as much as the delightful *valses* or dances of sensuous passion, has taught me about healing and guided my work as a doctor. Healing can only happen when you allow yourself to just *be* – and to experience in every instant just what you're supposed to experience.

When we listen to music, we allow the music to move us. It also guides the leader, who dictates the initiation and speed of the dance steps. As dancers evolve together, whether during one dance or over years of partnership, the embrace gives way to a surrender to both partner and music. If we're fortunate enough to dance to the accompaniment of a live orchestra, we can appreciate that its members, too, surrender – not only to one another as musicians, but to us, the dancers. Changing rhythms, enhancing crescendos, or expanding improvisational passages becomes a perpetual cycle of embrace, creation, and surrender.

Gorgeous melodies. Dancers gliding together as single, four-legged units. Elegant movements accentuating a musical motif – a *boleo* so perfect, I feel as if my toes are balanced upon the violinist's bow. A smoothly executed *sacada*. An exquisite *gancho*, placed as perfectly as an exclamation point in a suspense novel.

Then the song ends. The last notes melt into the air, and the dancing couples separate and walk toward their tables. The beautiful sounds and images are gone. We create the most tangible of art forms, yet these forms last but a few moments, vanishing along with the last musical note of a song. We create a memory.

And that memory leads to another, of watching Buddhist monks at the Cleveland Museum of Art creating a complex mandala made of colored sand. A succession of monks worked six hours a day for six days, placing vibrantly colored grains of sand one at a time with such precision that I was left breathless at the scope of the 8-square-foot task. The various intricate symbols depicted in the mandala were arranged with perfect symmetry.

On the seventh day, the monks ceremoniously swept away the sand, destroying their amazing work of art. Then the sand was taken to Lake Erie and cast over the waters. The entire ritual of creation and dispersion symbolized the lack of permanence in our existence. I was amazed by how hard the monks worked on their project and how they maintained their precision and focus, knowing that every moment they put into their work was bringing them that much closer to its ultimate destruction. Yet the monks worked with quiet joy, content in their respective roles and purpose.

And so it is with the dance. We begin the dance and bring joy to the act, knowing full well that it will eventually end. All things must pass. The dance has taught me that we cannot cling to anything or anyone. We cannot possess the things we most treasure.

If the dance is so impermanent, you may ask, why initiate the embrace in the first place? Why take risks that may lead only to brief, temporary successes or even to failure?

You may as well ask why we should want to be born, if life only culminates in death. It's not the destination that matters – it's the journey that fills us with wisdom and experience.

Let us come together and begin our journey. Will you walk with me?

GLOSSARY

Boleo: A woman's specialized back kick. This move is orchestrated by the leader when he creates centrifugal force in the direction of his partner's non-weight-bearing foot, which causes her foot to come off the floor while her knee remains still, preferably tightly opposed to her other knee. Her knee is the center, and as her lower leg swings around in the radius of a circle, her toes and heel trace an imaginary circle in the air. It is exquisite.

Cancion: Song. Some tangos are tango canciones, which are tangos that frequently contain passionate, romantic, or tragic lyrics.

Gancho (hook): A dancer kicks one leg around the partner's leg, against the thigh, so as to allow the lower leg to continue the arc, hooking the partner's thigh. The move is led by the man, since he needs to orchestrate and target the gancho. (Imagine what would happen if a woman just kicked up her heel between her partner's legs whenever she felt like it.) The woman should feel as though she's striking a match against the floor with the ball of her foot, generating an impulse that produces the lovely rapid-fire kick. Conversely, sometimes a gancho can be slow and held.

Milonga: A tango dance party. The term can also refer to a specific dance form, which has a quicker rhythm and lacks the languid foot drags of tango. It is reminiscent of a mazurka or polka.

Milonguero(a): A tango dancer; specifically one who dances in the milonguero style, particularly the style of "close embrace."

Sacada: A step in which the lead enters his partner's space with his leg or thigh, causing a displacement of her leg, which may create a sweep, a kick, or a change of direction.

Salon-style tango: Also referred to as *fantasia*, this Argentine tango style is the most frequently recognized at dramatic stage performances. This incorporates more figures and obviously requires more space between the partners and other dancers. (It's very impolite to dance salon style on a crowded dance floor.)

The Argentine tango is not to be confused with American, international, or ballroom tango. Argentine tango is the real deal. In my opinion, the other forms of tango are exhibition dances for onlookers. Argentine tango is an intimate and unchoreographed dialogue between two dancers. Onlookers are lucky to be present as voyeurs.

Tangueras: Female tango dancers.

Tangueros: Male tango dancers.

***Vals* or tango *vals*:** This is a form of tango with a time signature like that of the waltz. It clearly illustrates the marriage of Argentine tango with its very strong origins in European dance tradition.

Chapter 2

Do Not Anticipate

It's the universal rule for every tango dancer (specifically the woman or follower), and it should be the number one maxim for life: *Do not anticipate*. Unless you're the best psychic in the world, you'll rarely be correct when you try to second-guess your partner. (I say "rarely" because no one is wrong 100 percent of the time. Oops! I've just made an assumption.)

I want to emphasize the great difference between anticipating and being prepared. Put simply, I have found that people who anticipate carry around with them great expectations about how people will behave in certain situations, and when those expectations aren't met, they get frustrated or angry. This leads to disappointment. Do you let yourself become angered by the acquaintance who always shows up late? You expect that person to be punctual out of respect for your time, just as you respect hers. Yet she always arrives late, armed with an excuse. There was a long line at the gas station. Traffic was slow. She couldn't find a parking place. The cutest handbag was on display and she just had to get a second look at it … And all you can do is roll your eyes and think, *Caramba!*

On the other hand, when you're prepared you stay flexible and keep your eyes, ears, and other senses (including your sixth sense) open to all possibilities. And if you know your friend always comes late, be prepared – bring a book.

Anticipation is also the huge distraction that causes us to worry about every possible consequence of our actions or about all the possibilities that lie ahead of us. I'm convinced that anything beyond occasional worry is pathological and possibly a manifestation of depression.

For many, "do not anticipate" conjures an uncomfortable feeling of passivity or lack of control. On the contrary, this maxim reveals the potential for tranquil strength.

Let me show you what I mean. Ah, here comes the music.

Anticipation and the dance floor

The dance begins. Music surrounds me, enters me, beats with my heart, and flows through my veins. Moving to the music is so natural for my partner and me. Our dance steps click off without our even thinking of them. Then I detect a subtle change of weight and, without thinking, I follow his *salida* to the side. He performs a *sacada*, displacing my right leg, which provokes a long, beautiful sweeping motion on the floor. This voluptuous maneuver accentuates the introduction of the languid musical measures.

From the corners of my eyes, I see the crowd of spectators, thrilled to watch us perform. They like the way we performed the *sacada* so fluidly and think it's something we planned. But it wasn't. My partner suddenly had the idea to try something and I flowed with it so naturally that it seemed like an action we'd spent weeks rehearsing. If those observers only knew!

The audience anticipates more flashy showmanship as the music becomes more intense. But the irony is that I'm not allowed to anticipate, because a good *tanguera* isn't supposed to do that. In fact, I no longer want to know what is coming next. I block out the spectators – they no longer exist for me. I am my own audience. I just want to be in the moment and enjoy the dance.

Let me make this clear. Not anticipating *does not* mean that I just "wing it." Having no anticipation means that I'm very prepared – I come to the dance with inner strength and confidence in my ability to react to whatever situation arises. My confidence comes from self-assurance and discipline; I know that when I dance, I'm following my partner's lead, so that when he executes a move, I can flow along with it.

For example, if I detect that he wants to change the tempo, I may not know the exact move he's going to make, but I sense that something is coming; I feel his body preparing for the move. He may take a short breath, or he may do a hold. My awareness of him cues me. I need to be prepared, because something is going to change! I prepare myself – I don't anticipate. I don't think, *Okay, he's going to do a double-time.* He may not really launch a double-time. Maybe he wants to do a lift. And if I guess wrong – well, there goes our dance.

Here's another reason you shouldn't anticipate. Your movements might become too mechanical. When you start thinking to yourself, "He's going to do this, so I should do this, this, and this …," you end up concentrating so much on your feet that the dance stops flowing and instead becomes a series of footsteps. You might as well be playing hopscotch. You lose the artistic sense and become self-conscious, inhibited, and anxious because you're too busy wondering, *What is he going to do next? What is he about to pull out of his head?*

Men shouldn't anticipate either

Anticipation also can be wrong for the partner who leads. The leader can stagnate the dance when he begins making such calculations as *here's my move, and here's how the woman will follow.* And if she doesn't react in the way he expects her to, he may begin to stutter, like someone who loses his place during a speech. (That's why tango isn't a choreographed dance.)

The fact is, some men don't lead correctly, so our interpretation of what step they're attempting may be completely different from what the fellow had in mind. And when he doesn't get the response he was hoping for, he could choose to blame his partner. On the other hand, I've danced with some men who execute a move and expect step A, but instead get step B, and then later say to me, "Wow! You're the first dancer who's ever made that move! That is so cool! I'm going to make that one of my moves." And then we've got a new move, and we might go over it a few times and figure out all the different ways that we could vary that step. (As you can see, it isn't always the men who are from Mars or the women who are from Venus.)

Though the "do not anticipate" rule is aimed at women, it's similarly applicable to the fine leaders who realize that their own strength as leaders relies heavily upon their ability to solve problems. As I've said, we followers may interpret or follow the leads in different ways, ending certain steps in unanticipated positions. The wise tango leader sees these opportunities as ways to increase his repertoire, enjoying the challenge of disentangling himself and his partner and keeping the dance flowing.

You can't anticipate life

Having a firm idea in your mind of how someone should act or grow up doesn't just lead to hurt feelings. It can stunt the other person's emotional, intellectual, or spiritual growth – even if, in your heart of hearts, you love that person.

In my case, my path toward becoming a doctor wasn't anticipated. I'm the first person in my family on this side of the Mexican-American border to have a college degree. This side of the family couldn't fathom or support my dream and indeed found it rather arrogant of me to want to pursue higher education. The Mexican side of my family was less skeptical. Several men in our Mexican family were highly educated and, ironically, they were the ones who didn't look incredulously at me or laugh when I told them I had decided to become a physician. (For me, prejudice and sexism within my childhood home was a more formidable obstacle than any institutional or societal barrier I have encountered.)

Here's how it all began. As a preschool girl, I loved drawing the human form. The human body fascinated me and some of my sketches, based on models in art books, were quite graphic – so much so that before I entered Catholic school in first grade, my parents sat me down for a talk. They told me very gently that I did nice work, "but because you're going to the nun's school now, we would ask you just to be careful how you make your drawings. Keep clothes on your people, and don't make the boobs so big."

I also liked bugs. I used to chop up worms and in eighth-grade biology, I was one of the few girls who really enjoyed dissecting things. That's when I realized that I was different from the rest of the kids my age.

I loved science and math. Both my parents were math whizzes – Mom used to compete in national math contests in Mexico and my father was a mechanical engineer. But I was a little intimidated in school because all the other students had calculators. I once asked my father, who had a whole bureau of calculators, if I could have one. "No," he said, goading me into developing my intellectual muscles. "There's no way I'm going to have my daughter become lazy!" How about a slide rule, I begged. "No, you're not going to be lazy!" I was so embarrassed – I had to take honors physics without a calculator. Everyone else in my class had calculators and slide rules, and all I had was paper and pencils. On our first exam, I was the last one to finish. But by the end of the year, I was the first one done. And I won a physics honor prize that year!

During the commencement address given at my Catholic high school, the Mother Superior, a very attractive woman, said, "After going through all that education, I want one of you young women to be the first female President of this country." This was a bit of a revelation to me – after all, I had always been taught that little girls were meant to be seen and not heard. But from the ninth grade on, the progressive nuns at my all-girls high school told us things like "You'd better be self-sufficient" and "You'd better be able to support yourself. Because you don't know what's going to happen when you grow up. You can't anticipate whether you're going to be divorced or widowed or have children, so you'd better be prepared. You'd better be able to take care of yourself."

Then came the most illuminating moment in my life. While I was growing up, my father had told me that seeking a premed degree in college was silly – if I spent all my time in classes, labs, and morgues, I wouldn't be marriageable. At that time I was so sheltered that I thought, *Wow, maybe he's right.* Later, when I recounted that scene to one of my college counselors, her jaw dropped and she looked at me dumbfounded, as if to say, *What planet did you come from?*

When I saw that reaction from someone I really admired and respected, and then recalled everything I had heard from the nuns over the years, I was overwhelmed. I think it's the same for a lot of people who unquestioningly absorb all the prejudices and limitations of their parents and their cultures. My counselor said to me, "You have to pursue premed. You like it." And I said, "Yes, I've always wanted to be a doctor. It just never seemed to be the right thing to do because I'm a female." So I went on to premed, studied mummies, sold auto parts, became a doctor, and the rest is history. Or, should I say, *my* story.

A doctor's story

Years later, I relearned a very valuable lesson about the error of anticipation and stereotyping. A scruffy patient walked into the clinic and I immediately filed him under "long-haired-hippie-motorcycle-guy looking for disability compensation." He'd been injured as a result of a motorcycle accident and was undergoing rehabilitation. During his postoperative exams, it had been noted on his x-rays that he had calcifications in his prostate gland. This led to his consultation with me for presumed prostatitis.

He resumed full-time work as a mechanic in a southern Ohio town. During a follow-up visit, he came dressed in his work overalls and apologized that he hadn't had enough time to change between work and the appointment. He continued to suffer from severe lower-back pain but remained optimistic about finding the appropriate remedy.

When I saw him again three months later, he was pain-free. I was elated and, of course, curious about the successful remedy. He had tried everything, including anesthesia, pain therapy, and physical therapy, which were covered by his insurance. Unfortunately, none of those approaches seemed to work. Then, motivated by something he'd read, he tried acupuncture, paying for the treatment out of his own pocket. The results were completely successful.

As he happily recounted his experience, I listened to him in delighted surprise. My own ideas were being punctured, and I realized that we can't stereotype people on the basis of their looks. This unassuming, affable young man with the long hair had become my teacher. To this day, I still think about him, whenever I sense that I'm *anticipating*.

Becoming a dancer

Another thing to be aware of is – being aware. That is, if you spend your time anticipating what is yet to come, you stop paying attention to what's around you. You miss the signs and synchronicities that the universe is providing to alert you to possibilities for growth and change. And when you miss opportunities, you limit your options. After all, no one wants a life filled with signs that say "The Road Not Taken."

So don't worry about the future. It's already here. (Actually, we missed it – what we thought was the future has just become the past.)

I didn't anticipate being a dancer. I had no idea that the universe was preparing me for a vocation in dance. But I listened to my heart and paid attention to what life threw at me, and now dance is a great part of my life.

When I was younger, I danced for fun. I didn't know any steps; I just moved to music. I "molded" my steps into what my partner was doing. I think this is the way most people learn to dance. We just grow up dancing. But one thing I did notice. When I danced at family and social events, I could tell that I moved to rhythm as well as, if not better than, just about everyone around me.

Growing up, I never took formal or social or ballroom dancing classes. But on a lark, I took a class in classical ballet in college to fulfill a phys-ed requirement. That class, which mostly consisted of floor and bar exercises, was the first time I had to learn actual steps. That intrigued me. Ballet also helped me strengthen my torso and taught me how to hold my leg up higher. (Years later, I still use those bar exercises at home to limber up and maintain my agility so that I can keep dancing the tango.) I also loved the live piano accompaniment by the beautiful, raven-haired Russian woman whose playing swept me back to the time of Vaslav Nijinsky and Isadora Duncan. I loved it when she played Sergei Prokofiev's "March of the Montagues" during our exercises. Nothing beats dancing to live music.

I later took a master class in flamenco dancing, which made me appreciate the postures I learned in ballet. Flamenco is less restrictive than classical ballet. We could move more freely and improvise on the dance floor (much as we do with tango). In ballet, we had to bring our chest inward and pretend that our navel was pushed back to our spine. In flamenco, the posture was so different; for example, the chest was up and open. I really liked that completely immodest stance. It was freeing.

I began studying tango many years later, shortly after my divorce. Before my marriage, I went out dancing at least three days a week. (With such a schedule, I shocked my college classmates by graduating one year ahead of schedule!) I danced regularly for many years, but stopped just before I was married. After that I rarely had the opportunity to dance at social events, and we avoided nightclubs like the plague. I remember that after I pleaded for months to go out dancing, my then-husband and I went to a nice down-town club, but my excitement was quickly dampened by his numerous harsh complaints about the smoke, the loud music, the unsavory "element," and the "money-laundering" that was probably taking place. The fabulous rhythms and wonderful bass that had been pounding through my torso seemed to melt away, and I just wanted to go home and weep.

A few years later, as my speaking engagements increased and I began traveling more frequently, I realized that I could go out dancing again. At first, I felt incredibly guilty, as if I were becoming an adulteress. All I wanted was to dance! And I did; I made it a point to visit dance clubs in each new city I visited. These occasions were like religious retreats or spiritual re-energizers. But it wasn't until after my divorce that I had an epiphany as I was cooking in the tiny kitchen of my blighted farmhouse. "Oh my God! I'm free to dance – and dance all I want!" A few months later, the tango found me.

If you take a few moments and look back on your life, I bet you'll recognize the path that led you to where you are today. Was the road smooth or bumpy? What did you learn? Think about how the universe prepared you for your life. Would you like to change your life? We'll talk about that in a later chapter.

A metaphor for strength

Sally Potter, who directed and starred in the film *The Tango Lesson*, gives us these aphorisms, which get to the heart of "do not anticipate," an elementary rule of tango.

- To be alert enough to respond with the speed and precision required, the woman must keep her mind empty in the present moment.

- In order to surrender control of where she's going, she must be in complete control of her body.
- To be free enough to feel that she's flying, she needs to be completely grounded.

A private lesson I took with ballerina Anita Converse (of the late Cleveland Ballet) addressed the issue of anticipation. She demonstrated exercises to develop my inner strength and balance, including a very subtle maneuver involving weight transfer, which occurs just prior to the commitment of a step. This delicate maneuver features the transfer of one's weight from one foot to the other and takes place in slow motion, although the beat and the steps might be carried out rapidly. In this action, the nanoseconds of transfer become instances of suspense. With each step taken, in the deliberate pause between the commitment to the outstretched leg and the release of the supporting foot, endless opportunities arise for new steps and creativity.

This is also true of life. So much can happen between one footstep and the next. Give yourself the freedom to place your sole wherever you'd like. No expectations! There's no need to decide the rest of your life right now. Just be mindful of the instant before the transfer of weight and commitment. To paraphrase that famous twelve-step program, take it one footstep at a time.

Do you like the direction you're walking in?

Fear

Fear is another reason that we anticipate, suggests author and philosopher Deepak Chopra. Chopra cautions us about certain habits, such as completing other people's sentences. These habits, he believes, are signs of our need to control. And, ironically, it's weakness that compels us to grasp for control. This weakness comes from our inability to know our future and our fear of the unknown.

I'll share a secret with you. Even the most gifted psychics in the world will tell you that the messages they give don't always come to pass. That's because people can override any prediction by choosing to exercise their free will. Many people find the idea of free will exciting – it means that anything is possible. Unlimited possibilities! Indeed, I've given members of the Dr. Tango enterprise miniature sterling-silver kaleidoscopes engraved with the company motto "Infinite Possibilities."

Not everyone is so thrilled by the unknown. For many, this is where the fear factor comes in. If you feel as if there's no script or choreographed move into the future, you can't predict (or control) the outcome of your life – let alone what might happen tomorrow. So you start anticipating … and unfortunately, people who live in fear anticipate the worst. And the people who tend to overanalyze the past or overplan the future perpetuate the false concept of the present as mercurial, unstable, and therefore wasted. So the secret here is *don't* anticipate the future. Let it come to you. And be prepared, balanced, and alert.

Tango is a great way to extinguish the habit of anticipation. The dance is a metaphor of strength and an acceptance of whatever may come. More important, it sweeps us into the practice of being in the now. This happens whenever we step off the dance floor, entranced more by a feeling of accomplishment than by a memory of success.

GLOSSARY

Salida: The basic eight-step template from which all tango moves are derived. It's used as a teaching tool and also provides a language from which students or colleagues can communicate positions of initiation of closure.

Double-time: Taking two steps to one beat; going twice as fast.

Do "a hold": A pause; may or may not be associated with a stronger embrace.

Reverse *ocho*: One of the most fundamental building blocks of tango. It's a step defined as moving perpendicularly to the leader's direction, alternating from side to side; the partner initiates each new step by stepping behind herself. In the forward *ocho*, she again moves in alternating perpendicular directions but steps forward according to the leader's "invitation."

Chapter 3

The Stronger the Axis, the Fewer the Feet Needed on the Floor

Spinning out of control is a chaotic act. But twirling around your partner to create a flourishing dance step is adroit and artistic. Fancy footwork takes discipline. Chaos is the lack of discipline.

Actually, discipline is just part of the equation of dance. A partner must be prepared to act, must have a good sense of where his or her center of gravity is, and must know how to manipulate that space. After all, there's a world of difference between exquisitely executed *molinetes* and a game of Ring Around the Rosie.

Someone who spins chaotically has no sense of boundary. He's a bull in a china shop, upsetting whatever gets in his way, leaving a path of hurricane-style destruction, the kind that uproots trees and brings down power lines. People like this who are out of control – addicts of every ilk, as well as physical and emotional abusers – must be avoided, lest they crash into you and end up doing something to upset or uproot your life.

What's tough, though, is when the person who's out of control is someone you care about. I know this sounds cruel, but people who upset you because they have addictive problems they're not willing to face must be avoided until they're ready to accept help. Others, however, who are stumbling about in their self-made darkness yet truly are seeking some light, may be helped. But how do you give support to someone in need without losing your balance or hurting yourself in the process?

It takes patience, trust, and flexibility to spin on your axis because you must carry added weight. That's why it's important to know your center of gravity as well as how much weight you can displace without falling on your bottom.

The tango lesson

I once watched tango dancers Diego Di Falco and Carolina Zokalski demonstrate simultaneous and alternating *ochos* (figure eights) with *sacada* displacements. This was especially challenging when Carolina was executing high kicks or *sacadas*: Two of the dancers' four feet had to remain on the floor, and the success of the step relied on the axis of the couple, which stretched from head to toe.

Basically, a *sacada* is a displacement of the non-weight-bearing leg. Low *sacadas* can cause subtle sweeps or lifts. High *sacadas*, usually initiated at the level of the thigh, can be more dramatic because they involve higher kicks and longer strides, depending upon inertia and the partner's ability and agility.

I once watched two dancers from the Tango Buenos Aires dance company execute the following amazing step, which simply illustrates the axis of a couple at its very best. The two dancers had only one of their four feet on the dance floor as the man, in one of the most sophisticated leads I've ever seen, ushered his partner onto the top of his foot. As he bent his knee and lifted her off the ground, she balanced and pivoted on the ball of her foot. He then pivoted on his weight-bearing leg, and ended the step with her landing smoothly on her previously non-weight-bearing foot and closed into a *media luna*.

Brava! The lift was unexpected and the couple executed it effortlessly; lovingly, in fact. I caught my breath as the woman appeared to tower over her partner and maintain a vertical, featherlike posture. I watched attentively, trying to figure out how they had accomplished that move, hoping the leader would do it again. I was eager to see how they had set up the maneuver. But like a magician, this performer wouldn't repeat the trick. He wouldn't reveal the secret to the eager students in attendance, nor would he give in to audience prompting.

Later, Carolina explained in her charming Porteña accent (the accent of a Spanish speaker from Buenos Aires) the balance both partners need to execute their maneuvers in unison. If the axis between the couple is strong, she said, they're able to have fewer feet on the floor. In other words, a couple with a strong shared axis would be able to maintain their balance even in the absence of four-point footing. Carolina was teaching a class in *sacadas*, and this was an especially challenging lesson about double *sacadas*: two feet – one his, one hers – came off the floor simultaneously. The move was a test of balance, sensitivity, trust, and weight placement, because you cannot execute a *sacada* if your balance isn't good to begin with.

The importance of balance

The center of balance is in the torso and pelvis – specifically the spinal musculature, which is balanced upon the weight-bearing leg. This isn't often obvious to the eye, but it's very obvious to the dancers. The leader cannot successfully displace the follower if he's not aware of the weight-bearing side of the follower's body; he can only do a *sacada* if he senses that the follower's weight has shifted so it can be supported by the opposite leg that he's going to displace.

The act of displacing somebody requires great sensitivity. Being a leader is a privilege; it takes a great deal of responsibility to execute a *sacada*. If you displace the wrong leg, you can literally knock your partner down. If you're kicking someone's leg out from beneath her, you have to know before you kick her leg that she's prepared to accept that action.

A *sacada* isn't planned out beforehand. Good dancers know how their partners feel; with an adept leader, I can sense his shift of weight and he can kick my leg with gusto. But I'm advanced enough so that if a leader kicks his leg out and I lose my balance, it's really my fault. (But that's a secret, because a woman is never at fault in tango.)

It bears repeating that there's a lot of trust involved in this step – trust that the leader knows what he's doing and trust that if he performs this move correctly, the follower will respond accordingly. Because this maneuver can be quite risky, I will not perform it with a first-time dancer. Well, usually not …

Let me tell you about a fellow I once met, whom I will call "Tom the Turk." At a social event, Tom, a stranger, asked me to dance. He said I looked very poised. (Nice opening line.) Since it was our first time together, I expected that he'd step on my toes a few times, maybe there'd be a slight attempt at a flourish, and then he'd make a polite bow at the end of our dance.

The music started. He placed his arms around my shoulders and back to create a gentle cradle, and I took a polite step back, letting him know how much space between us I was comfortable with. His lead was deliberate and firm. I felt safe and very confident in his lead.

The next thing I knew, I was towering over his head. The ball of my foot was on top of his foot and he lifted up his leg and led me into a pivot. I pivoted on top of his shoe, my leg out; he pivoted, double-pivoted, and then gracefully set me down. I got off on my foot, then finished the maneuver by turning around into a *molinete*. This was the same move I had seen on stage … and now I knew that it wasn't a magic trick after all. I was awestruck. Where had he learned that step?

I whispered in his ear, *Can you do that again?* (Ouch! That was really bad tango etiquette – do not anticipate! But could you blame me for wanting more?) He waited until a moment in the next dance when I was no longer anticipating. Indeed, I had already released the possibility from my mind and once again his maneuver came as a fantastic surprise.

Later I asked Tom, "How did you know you could do that with me?" He smiled coolly and answered, "I just knew. I could feel that you were prepared to do it." (Thank goodness he thought I was so poised.) The statement Carolina had made in that sultry dance studio several summers ago came immediately to mind: "The stronger the axis of the couple, the fewer feet you need on the floor."

Developing the axis

How do we develop such an axis? How do we become one agile unit?

During the workshops I present for corporations or teaching institutions, I often ask participants to imagine their families, their classrooms, and their businesses as a single animal with many legs … perhaps as an exotic insect. The body of such a creature must be strong and balanced in order to endure displacement of its few or many feet. Each member contributes to the strength and balance of the whole, which must be unified in some way. Something has to hold the parts together, whether it's a mission statement, a spiritual philosophy, or a religion.

Did you know that most married couples never engage in such intimate discussions? According to Kathy Dawson, a relationship coach based in Northeast Ohio, 75 percent of couples who marry in a church don't converse about their religious beliefs in the course of their marriage. If we're not discussing such fundamental topics within the context of our most precious and intimate relationship, what can we expect to befall family, schools, and business? Our core spiritual beliefs are the framework upon which we build the axis for each team and partnership.

I think of the *sacadas*, those various displacements of feet and legs, as the challenges or crises we meet during our life journeys. How strong are the axes we have formed with others? Are we doing our share of nurturing and fortifying each axis through the time we spend honestly listening to others? Do we really share a religious faith or are we just going through the motions? Are we trustworthy?

Tango has made me realize that we needn't remain vulnerable to life's *sacadas*. We need only be mindful of our spiritual purpose, our objectives, and the love we surrender for the good of that four-legged animal we become when we dance.

Sometimes it hurts to help

Here's a different kind of story about risk, balance, and sensitivity. While I was trying to help women in the Third World, I underwent a crisis of faith. The experience left a bitter taste in my mouth, but I truly believe it made me a stronger person.

I graduated in 1983 from the Lake Erie College for Women with a liberal arts degree with concentrations in foreign language, fine art, and biology. Part of me wanted to fly straight into medical school, but then I won an ITT

Fellowship. I thought it would be interesting to take some time off and study mummies in a small town where the residents still believed in witchcraft and bedevilment. (More about that later.)

Since I was thinking about applying to medical school, I decided to volunteer at the *Instituto Seguro Social del Estado* clinic, a small medical facility that served the mostly poor people of the country. At the clinic I drew blood, observed surgery, and spent time in the pathology lab. The pathologist, who drew Pap smears and diagnosed such conditions as trichomonas, was curious about the prevalence of sexually transmitted disease in the region, so we began testing for STDs with every Pap smear.

But the sad thing is that when we found an infected woman, we weren't allowed to tell her about her disease because it would create a scandal in her marriage. (Nor could I dispense birth-control pills.) Many infected women went untreated. Their husbands were fooling around and passing infections to their wives. Once, I tested one of my fellow nurses and when the results came back positive, I asked her whether she wanted treatment. I was stunned by her reaction. "That son of a bitch," she said. "I keep getting treated over and over again, and he keeps reinfecting me."

Not to be able to treat these women patients was so frustrating. Many had traveled great distances over hard dirt roads to obtain this medical attention. I felt caught in a tough balancing act. I was very vocal about how we were betraying these women; everyone at the clinic knew how I felt. But I didn't want to be kicked out of the hospital, so I had to step back and realize that this was a culture where STDs would have gone undetected anyway. In this culture a woman was probably going to be reinfected, and she wouldn't get divorced over it. Men were expected to behave in a certain way, and women in another.

Besides, we weren't testing for herpes or HIV; in 1983, it wouldn't have been possible to test that population for HIV. What we were looking for wasn't fatal: gonorrhea, chlamydia, yeast infections, and trichomoniasis. Most STDs in women are asymptomatic; that is, they become pelvic inflammatory diseases which, in some instances, manifest as chronic pelvic pain. Often, the result is infertility because with so much scar tissue, the uterus becomes basically useless. So for some of these women, there was a cruel irony – they couldn't get birth-control pills. (Or doctors were not allowed to tie their tubes without their husband's consent.) Maybe it was a blessing in disguise that STDs curtailed their ability to conceive – most women no longer wanted to anyway.

This experience led to my rather long hiatus away from the Catholic Church. Back then, I was naïve; I thought I could educate these women about family planning, the rhythm method, and other things. I urged the local gynecologist to start performing tubal ligations; shocked, he said we needed the husband's consent. I was appalled. These women were being beaten for telling their husbands that they didn't want intercourse when they were ovulating, and we weren't allowed to give them birth-control pills. Women with eight kids were begging to have their tubes tied while their children were dying of malnutrition. At the same time, the Pope came to Mexico and told everyone that birth control was a sin.

I just couldn't stand the hypocrisy anymore. It was a sin to prevent conception by means of a prophylactic or a pill, but it was okay to avoid pregnancy by plotting graphs, taking a daily temperature, and going to great lengths to avoid making love when it was possible to conceive. Are we so primitive that we can attribute sin to an act but not to mindful strategies intended to meet the same objective?

This was a painful dilemma. I had gone to Catholic school for twelve years and I loved the nuns. Yet I felt in an ugly way that I was betraying the women coming to the clinic by being so Catholic and not showing them any compassion. I felt like one of those innocent, sheltered, liberal suburbanites who become bleeding-heart social workers. What right did I have to burst into this culture and upset the way life had been lived for hundreds of years? Was I helping women by forcing a whole new lifestyle upon them? Would I actually be hurting them more by displacing them in their culture? I needed to step back.

One woman who had been able to get birth-control pills hid them under her mattress. But her husband found them and beat her.

The story of Viviana y Isodoro

Fortunately, there are stories of trust and balance that do have happier endings.

I met Viviana and Isodoro several years ago when they were conducting a weekend of tango workshops. The two reside in Washington, D.C., but they were born in Argentina. They left their homeland not as adventurous young people but as married partners with three children. They spoke no English and no host family awaited them in the United States. Yet they decided to take the extraordinary risk of uprooting themselves in order to give their children a better future.

The couple pursued a number of ventures. Their successful auto-repair shop enabled the family to thrive in their new country. On a lark, they began taking ballroom dancing classes, and their love of dancing became so great that it influenced their family life. One of their daughters joined Madonna's dance troupe. I enjoyed seeing the proud gleam in Isodoro's eyes as he described the excitement of seeing his daughter dancing onstage with "The Material Girl." (Wow! This had been one of my own fantasies ever since I became addicted to music videos in the early 1980s.)

When we met, I was surprised to learn that Viviana and Isodoro had been dancing tango for only eight years. He, a handsome 50-something man who stood about 5-foot-3, moved athletically as his partner, plump and coquettish, playfully embellished his every physical nuance. The couple delighted students with their ageless sexiness and whimsy. The two embodied the strong axis that can be forged between a pair of committed *tangueros* as well as the shared axis most married couples would find enviable. When they decided to *jump*, they were aware of their mutual strength and the bond it formed between them. They were not confined by convention or fear.

Taking chances requires balance on the weight-bearing leg and liberation of the other limbs from gravity. If a couple has a strong axis, the partners are able to kick, spin, *gancho*, and *sacada* together. They can trust and support each other; as one dreams, the other will work to make that dream reality. They can also inspire each other to create even more spectacular dance maneuvers. And they can have fun.

GLOSSARY

Alternating *ochos* with *sacadas* (displacements): (See definition of *ochos* on page 38.) With every other *ocho*, the leader can perform a *sacada* against his partner's non-weight-bearing leg. He can also create an illusion by which he leads her to perform a *sacada* against him.

Double *sacadas*: This occurs when the man performs a *sacada* against the woman's leg and also creates a *sacada* against himself, causing simultaneous displacement of both dancers. If the *sacadas* are performed with a bit more gusto – "high *sacadas*" – both dancers will be balancing upon one foot each while their other feet leave the floor.

***Media luna*:** This step is similar to an *ocho cortado*, except that the partner collects her feet and pivots, taking an additional step before returning to position in front of her partner.

***Molinete* (pinwheel):** In a *molinete*, a series of steps leads the woman around the man as though he were the axis of a wheel. This is carried out by the follower, who alternates front, side, back, and side steps while paying special attention to posture and pivoting technique. The step can be greatly embellished with intermittent *sacadas* and performed by the leader, who steps into the woman's open steps as they turn.

Ocho cortado: This is a short or truncated figure eight. In this step, the leader invites the woman to step toward his right side with her right foot, then leads her into a side step with her left foot. As he syncopates, he brings his partner back in front of him as she pivots and drags her left foot to a cross in front of her right.

Chapter 4

Ochos Aren't Always Figure Eights

We're all part of the eternal dance of life. We begin as our parents' children and we look with pleasure toward our grandparents. Then we become parents to our children and later look forward to spending time with and giving pleasure to our grandchildren …

We take so many major steps on the journey called "life." Along the way, each big move is built from smaller steps. As we grow from childhood to adulthood, we make friends, lose friends, take jobs, find better jobs, fall in and out of love, seek the soul mate we just *know* is out there. And so we dance through life, just as our ancestors did and just as our descendents will.

The doctor in me sees the infinity sign – a reclining figure eight – as the double helix representing the DNA inherited from our forefathers that we will pass to future generations *ad infinitum*. But the dancer in me sees the infinity sign as an *ocho*, a dance step that literally means "eight" in Spanish. The *ocho* is a classic step, timeless and beautiful in its simplicity. It's a primary step that dancers can build on. And it's a step that will last forever.

Performing the *ocho*

Here's how to perform an *ocho*. The man draws the woman to his side, then syncopates and pulls her to his other side. Then he keeps moving her around him in a perpendicular fashion, creating the pattern of figure eights made by her steps on the dance floor. That's the classic *ocho*.

A reverse *ocho* happens when the man takes his partner into a side step, then syncopates again to the side while directing his chest in the same manner, which causes his partner to pivot and step. This can lead the partners into performing a series of alternating and swiveling steps.

Indeed, an *ocho* is defined as any step made by the follower that is perpendicular to the leader's direction or vertical step. However, the *ocho* isn't a true side step – the woman is stepping either directly backward or forward, crossing in front of the man's forward or backward direction.

The *ocho* is the foundation of tango dancing. It's a basic step – a bridge step that can also be used as a building block. You could use the move to initiate a change of direction. Or you could build from that move into sumptuous *sacadas*, delightful *molinetes*, or any number of other steps. It's a good leadoff step that will help you understand the dynamics of pivoting and moving on the dance floor. And when you can't advance in the line of dance, it provides a good way to pause so that you don't crash into other dancers – you can just keep the eights coming and coming.

Ochos can be fun. I remember a class I took with El Pulpo – "The Octopus." (It's an appropriate moniker for a dancer whose legs behave like tentacles, intertwining with the legs of his dance partners in some of the most intricate steps I've ever experienced.) One of his classes was titled *Ocho Loco* – Crazy Eights. He taught us a move of his own invention, *ochos* led and carried out from the opposite leg into the opposite direction. To a traditional dancer, this seemed like heresy, but then he had us combine these in alternating fashion with the traditional *ocho* – and, oh, what fun we had, creating patterns containing new pauses and pivots!

A word of caution, however. Don't dismiss the *ocho* as a trifle. It's not just a series of figure eights. *Ochos* are things you can build on, just as if you were using knowledge from the past to create a better today and an even grander tomorrow.

Learning from the past

Sometimes past experiences are so profound, they form a living background to everything that follows, resonating forever after. Sometimes they give rise to a mood, an attitude, a sense of awe, that becomes permanently ingrained. Such was my experience in Guanajuato.

As I mentioned previously, I won a grant to pursue the question of why the corpses buried in the small Mexican town of Guanajuato decomposed slowly and took on the look of mummies. My plan was to open up the crypts and interview people to get their reactions to the mummies. Behind my back, several people accused me of being a necrophile. They felt that I was being very disrespectful. I understand why they felt that way, but I never intended to show disrespect. I was studying this phenomenon in a scientific way.

Rumor had it that the unusual preservation of the bodies occurred because of the minerals in the soil. Guanajuato was a mining town, and the environment was dry. Two of the mummies were the remains of two French physicians who died in the late 1800s; they and a *charro* (a Mexican cowboy) were the only ones with their clothes on. All the rest were nude.

Here's how the mummies were discovered. In the late 1800s, the town imposed a one-year perpetuity on crypt purchases; if a family did not pay for its crypt in that year, the body buried there would be exhumed and cremated. Well, when cemetery workers started opening crypts, they were surprised to find intact bodies. Instead of disposing of these mummified remains, they took them to the ossuary, which was a floor beneath the cemetery. (Think of the catacombs below Rome.)

The route to the ossuary was very dramatic. You had to walk through the cemetery, then move a stone on the grounds out of the way of a spiral staircase, which you descended carrying a candle. Once below, you were surrounded by dozens of mummies. It could be pretty frightening.

The locals charged tourists to visit the ossuary, and legends sprang up about visitors whose shawls got caught in the mummies, trapping them underground, where they died.

During the 1960s, the mummies were placed in a "museum." This consisted of a long hallway housing a row of several hutches in which the desiccated bodies were exhibited.

The mummies unnerved area residents, who believed that mummification was the work of the devil. They feared that if the bodies of their loved ones mummified, they'd be stolen and put in the museum. There were stories of family members who attended exhumations in order to dismember intact bodies and prevent the corpses from going on display for tourists. What a repellent fate! Imagine living in a small town and knowing that there was a possibility that after your death your body would be exhibited and talked about by the idly curious.

Sometimes I watched these exhumations. I have to admit that I felt a morbid curiosity. More than once, I took a photographer to the cemetery after it closed and gained entrance by bribing the night watchman with chocolates from the United States. We'd enter the museum, take out the mummies, and photograph them. They weighed nothing. It was like lifting cardboard. Their backs were completely straight.

Sometimes we forgot which mummy went where and put them back in the wrong places. The next day, the tour guides freaked out when they found that the mummies weren't where they'd been the day before.

Working with the mummies made me realize how some people's lives revolve around their appearance and how once you die you have no control over how you'll be seen by others. (As the saying goes, "Funerals are not for the dead, they're for the living.")

Most of the mummies were the remains of people who had died in their 60s or 70s, but occasionally we encountered the remains of a young woman who had died in childbirth. You could tell the approximate age of a woman when she died by her breasts. When a woman's breasts were sunken rather than wrinkled, you could tell that they had once been big and full, and had therefore belonged to a young woman.

You could also tell which corpses were those of young men – their chests were sunken rather than sagging and atrophied, and you could imagine that such a body had belonged to a person who had once been healthy and shapely. Viewing a younger corpse always gave rise to a sense of tragedy; one inevitably wondered what had happened to rob that person of life.

I also found myself wondering whether the souls of any of these people were still lingering in the vicinity. I hoped that if they were, what I was doing wouldn't strike them as disrespectful.

That concern was brought home to me one night during a severe thunderstorm. I was in the narrow corridor that defined the "museum," sketching a mummy in an attempt to discern what he would have looked like when he was alive. I was sitting in a chair before the corpse, and suddenly all the lights went out.

The darkness was so complete that I felt dizzy. I felt the room tipping and imagined that all the mummies were going to slide and fall on me. My heart began pounding and I said to the darkness, "You know, I don't mean any harm. I don't mean any disrespect." Somehow that made me feel better.

I often carried my tape recorder so that I could collect impressions of the mummies from local citizens. During one bus ride, I sat beside a middle-aged woman of very humble means and asked her to share her thoughts about living in a city where one might be destined to be mummified after death. She agreed to talk.

At first she was hesitant, but then she mustered the courage to speak. She asked whether I'd seen the infant mummy, which was dressed like San Martin de Porres. (It was customary to dress dead babies as saints as a form of solace and homage.)

I did indeed remember that little mummy very well. He was exhibited in the hutch that was reserved for the smaller mummies and was richly costumed in lace and green velvet. "He is my son," she said, her voice trembling. "I could not afford the perpetuity. And I haven't the money to get him out of the museum, though I tried very hard so many years ago."

The bus jerked us forward and back as the loud motor shifted gears and strong diesel fumes stung our nostrils. Several strands of wavy hair stuck to the woman's cheeks and forehead. In spite of the sultry afternoon sun, I was immobilized by a helpless chill. She averted her eyes from my gaze, excused herself, and left the bus. Moments later, I realized that I had not even asked the child's real name.

Learning for the future

The mummies were a constant reminder to the residents of Guanajuato that the past was always with them. Today, even with my solid career in medicine, when I think about the human body, I remember what I learned from my experiences in Guanajuato. We can be strong, we can be fragile. And the cycle of life has no beginning or end.

I was especially aware of this throughout my pregnancy. During my first trimester, questions went through my mind. Where did I come from? What made me feel that I was worthy of reproducing myself? Add to those worries the fact that I was a medical student and knew all the things that could possibly go wrong from here to delivery.

But I surrendered my fears to the realization that giving birth is the greatest leap of faith that a human being can make. I would accept the responsibility of becoming a parent, and I would help my child develop into a complete individual.

Well, child-rearing doesn't get easier. My old concerns are gone, but new worries have arisen in their place. Now that my children are in their teens, I find myself once again wondering what comes next.

I realized the other day that I can't answer this question. Only my children can. Their lives are now their own. A friend of mine once said, "We don't own our children, we just rent them." Let's hope they use what we taught them to make good, responsible decisions. Because when you get right down to it, our children owe us nothing. We must stop worrying about them. They're completely independent and free to go out and join the world.

Being a parent is our greatest contribution to the process of evolution. In my opinion, this is a divine act. We perfect future generations through our children. This is what makes evolution a sacred process.

When I imagine the infinity sign, I'm reminded of what inspired me to become a doctor. Remember the television program *Ben Casey*? (He was the 1960s version of Dr. McDreamy.) The infinity sign was used in the program's opening credits. Every time I look at the dance floor after practicing figure eights, I see in the path of those simple, basic steps a panorama of infinity signs.

A lesson for tango

However, things are not always what they seem. I may study the scratches on my wooden floor after a heavy solo *ocho* workout and see many figure eights (or expanding sequences of infinity symbols). Other times, the scratches on the floor may just represent a vigorous, satisfying workout.

Tioma Malorasky, one of my favorite tango teachers, said, "Elegance is the efficiency of movement." I believe he means that grace comes from ease and simplicity of movement.

Many tango moves that look contorted or forced aren't really that way at all. When you move your body in the way it was meant to move – when you have good posture, good awareness, and good balance – you can actually execute such moves easily.

Nothing is sloppy, and no gesture is a wasted movement. And efficiency in any setting – whether in dance, work, or life – is elegance.

So take the dance one step at a time. To do that, get back to the basics – the building blocks of what dance is all about. And in the case of tango, the building block is the *ocho*. Get that right, and you can use it to create anything you want.

GLOSSARY

Syncopation: This shift of accent in a passage of music occurs when a normally weak beat is emphasized. It is used to modify musical rhythm.

Chapter 5

Always Keep Your Heart in Front

During a recent tango workshop, we were asked to experiment with different methods of leading. We led each other from the head, from the nose, from the knees, and from the feet.

For example, when told to lead from his nose, the leader was inclined to stand with his face in front of his body, inviting his partner to assume different positions by pointing his nose in different directions. In another example, when instructed to lead from their feet, men leaned back slightly and tried to coerce their partners' legs and feet into different places. This quickly limited the repertoire!

Each exercise, with its own postures, aesthetics, and communication, helped us realize how difficult it was to lead. But the exercises also enhanced our appreciation of a *true* lead. For that, you lead from the heart.

When leading from the heart, the man focuses the energy of his intention in his chest. Similarly, the follower responds through her own heart, making every effort to maintain the position of her heart in front of his throughout the dance. This is particularly challenging when a couple executes a *molinete*, where the woman is led around her partner as though he were the axle of a wheel. She performs her part by stepping, pivoting hard, and stepping again. All the while, her chest is parallel to his. And at times her waist and hips carry her legs to a point perpendicular to his shoulders.

When you're learning this step, leading (or being led) may seem like an exaggerated, unnatural move, but when it is done properly and with the correct balance, it should be effortless.

Through this exquisite dance a man is asked to become whole – to be a person who can think and communicate through his heart. At the same time, tango challenges women to recapture the essence of their femininity by opening their hearts and listening to the beat of the music that flows through their partner's heart.

The "three-minute marriage"

Keeping your heart in front of your partner's means letting your heart guide you. For the woman, it means assuming a posture that allows her to effectively receive the lead. It means being chest to chest, or *ventrum* to *ventrum*. Visualize two hearts beating in rhythm. The challenge is to do this as he leads the *molinete*, when he's the axis of the circle. The woman must travel around him and pivot very aggressively at the waist and torso in order to make the movement fluid, yet remain in contact, chest to chest.

Some tango dancers refer to each dance as a "three-minute marriage." That's because if it weren't for the dance, most men and women wouldn't find themselves in such close proximity. If the couple were to meet under other circumstances, they wouldn't gaze into each other's eyes or hold each other around the waist or stand heart to heart – well, at least not until the third or fourth date. But when new couples meet to embrace on the dance floor, they're allowed to be as close as they find comfortable.

Not only that, but the dance creates trust in the leader. You're allowing him to lead you. The man has to be trusting, too. He trusts that you'll follow his steps and complement the dance he's trying to create. You keep building on each other's trust, step after step, and the relationship evolves over the three minutes of the dance. You get to know each other. As he learns your response time, your agility, and what your stride is like, you learn about your partner – what steps he likes, how he leads, if he likes to hold tightly, and so forth.

How do you create a good three-minute marriage? By not anticipating. By leaving yourself open for whatever may happen and exposing yourself as you'd expose your artwork or sing in public. It's like letting someone see you naked, and you trust that the exposure will be respected, valued, and cherished. The dance has to be cherished, too; otherwise, the marriage – whether it lasts three minutes or for a lifetime – isn't likely to work.

Good business sense

Leading with your heart is an apt metaphor for the things that guide us in our lives. When it comes to the business world, successful leaders know this rule: "Find your mission, and the profit will follow." In other words, start an enterprise with a good intention instead of purely to make money, and you'll find true success. People who are guided by their hearts believe that creating happiness and giving service to others is more important than making scads of money.

An effective leader is one in whom people recognize passion and integrity. Former Secretary of State Colin Powell said that people lose faith in their leader when they believe he or she is incompetent, ineffectual, or untrustworthy. True leaders are those who engender trust and practice a lifestyle that brings value into the workplace. By that, I don't mean that good leaders are preachy or moralistic, but that they're genuine and their passion for success is contagious. They lead with their hearts.

Sometimes I hear people say that the business environment needs more intellect and less emotion. Well, I believe that being too intellectual will sabotage your gut-level intuition. Unfortunately, when people think of someone as emotional, they imagine him or her as someone who flies off the handle, or regularly gets angry or becomes sentimental. Angry or sentimental people do not lead with their hearts – they lead by fear. Avoid these people. Being heart-smart means using your intuition, acting from a moral core, and respecting others.

Someone once asked me, "As a doctor and as a leader, how do you find happiness in what you're doing?" I thought about that for a moment and then laughed. "I don't find happiness," I said. "It just bites me in the nose."

Heart happiness

Patients regularly tell me that I'm the only doctor who smiles. Now, I'm sure there are plenty of other physicians who smile and have a pleasant demeanor. And my patients are not among the happiest in the hospital – I see my share of critically sick and dying people. But I refuse to be a somber person.

My secret? I have no secret. People appreciate being able to touch me. They respect me because I'm accessible. Patients aren't afraid of me. And when they reach out to hug me, they get a hearty hug in return.

At the same time, not all patients want to be touched, physically or metaphorically. I always respect a patient's needs and desires.

Here's a case in point, the story of a fellow I'll call "Ed." Ed's face was damaged and scarred when he saw action in World War II, and children found it frightening. His rough appearance gave rise to a rough personality, yet he was a very sensitive and intelligent man. He traveled from his large farm in southern Ohio to our urology clinic for treatment of his prostate cancer, but he never allowed me to examine him. He made it very clear that he was rather old-fashioned and modest. He respected me, but he just couldn't allow himself to undergo physical examination conducted by a woman. Yet he wasn't afraid to ask very pointed questions about sexuality. *Whoa!* We made each other smile.

Once Ed's wife accompanied him on a visit to me, and told me, "I can't believe he won't let you examine him, but I can assure you, he absolutely adores you. He has the greatest respect for you." He just couldn't cross that threshold. He talked to me about everything from his favorite books to all the platoon buddies he had lost in battle during World War II. Meanwhile, I continued to monitor lab work, review studies performed before we met, and look at x-rays from his hometown hospital. As his disease progressed, he developed androgen-resistant cancer, which meant that the only treatment option was chemotherapy.

When I told him that, he thought for a moment and then said that he didn't want to have chemotherapy.

Later, he asked me, "How do you think I'll die?"

That stopped me cold. I outlined the different scenarios I thought could lead to his death and told him that I was hoping for his sake that he'd die of renal failure, so that he could die in his sleep.

He took my statement very well. It had been very hard for me to say. Even for a doctor, it's often difficult to talk to a patient about death. It's so much easier to talk about helping people get better. But Ed trusted me and asked an honest question, and I honored his trust with an honest answer. He deserved to get back what he had given me. I followed his lead, and we danced heart to heart.

There is no failure

When I was 12 years old, my grandfather died of metastastic prostate cancer. The following night, I slept in the bed where he died, while my grandmother slept down the hall. At least she wouldn't be alone in their old farmhouse.

While my grandfather was dying, no one in my family ever talked to him directly about his impending death. He was a very smart man – I believe he knew what was happening to him, yet no one ever let him talk about dying or about how to arrange his affairs. Whenever he tried to raise the subject, family members would dismiss him with the excuse that they were protecting his feelings. In my opinion, that was just plain cowardice. My grandfather died lonely because no one would let him talk about himself.

Later, when we cleaned his room, we found dozens of pills on the floor between his bed and the wall. It was tragic; he was probably spitting out the pills the doctors were giving him because he thought that the medication was meant to extend his life. But some of the pills he was spitting out were pain pills. He endured so much pain, yet no one ever told him the purpose of those pills he was dumping beside his bed.

Whenever it feels difficult to refer a patient to hospice, I remember my grandfather. While the patient is usually okay with the decision, the family is often angry because they think I'm stifling their hope. But of course that's not my intention. I'm respecting the patient's wishes.

My grandfather was a bright man, the pillar of the family. Everyone came to him for advice, money, or help. And yet he died stripped of dignity, much less authority. Hospice patients want that last bit of control over their life. Even while family members appear to be trying to be helpful and encouraging by saying things like, "Oh, no, you'll get better," they're really just protecting themselves and pushing the patient away.

Still, when it comes to recommending hospice, there's a part of me that feels that I am giving up. Sometimes it's hard not to see death as a failure on our part. Doctors enter this profession thinking that we're going to heal all people. So it feels as if I'm letting patients down when I have to be realistic and tell them that the treatment just isn't working.

Pediatric oncologist Naomi Remen, author of *Kitchen Table Wisdom*, addresses this. She writes that medical school teaches us not to get emotionally involved with patients because involvement would lead to burnout. However, she believes that keeping our distance from patients ultimately leads to more burnout, because we end up practicing denial. So while I have a very low threshold for tears, I have no threshold for crying – in fact, I'm grateful for that, because weeping is probably the very thing that keeps me from feeling burnt out. Tears make me feel alive, and for me it's a privilege to share such strong emotions in such an intimate way with another human being.

One more thought on this subject. Death is *not* a failure. In medicine, we often say that the patient failed, as if to imply that *we*, as doctors, didn't fail – it was the *patient* who failed. Why not say the treatment failed? Or, better yet, why even use the word at all?

Mr. P.

Here's the story of another patient who honored me with his life. Mr. P. let me know that he was going to die lonely. He was afraid to ask his lover to be at his side.

For many years, Mr. P. traveled from his home in India to Cleveland Clinic for cardiology and urology checkups. His adult children accompanied him. Unfortunately, their arrogance and demanding behavior could not be disguised as doting on their father.

A modest gentleman, Mr. P. surprised me the first time he asked to discuss "certain matters" out of earshot of his children. He was concerned about his sexual ability. Despite numerous medical problems and a lengthy list of medications, he cared about his erectile function and his ability to satisfy his lover. He had been widowed over twenty years earlier, so his children, who had no knowledge of his lover, couldn't fathom their father's concern.

During his last visit, again he asked his children to leave the room. As usual, I was glad to see them go. But when we were alone, I was stunned by his words.

"I am dying," he said quietly. "I know this."

He reviewed the results of his recent heart tests and the conclusions made by his doctors here and in India. His condition, he said, was deemed terminal and inoperable.

"You know, doctor, I am going to die alone." His eyes were moist and his voice was soft. "I never imagined it would be this way."

"But you have your children," I said, almost half-heartedly. "What do you mean, alone?"

"You see, doctor, twenty-three years ago, I was struggling with my heart. My dear wife traveled everywhere with me, caring for me during a two-year ordeal, which led to my surgery. All the while, she silently suffered. I didn't know. She was so quiet and loving. Her kidneys failed. I desperately returned her to the place where they had saved my life. But it was too late."

He recounted the pain of his loss and his remorse at being unable to reciprocate the care she had so willingly given him. Shyly, then, he spoke of how years later he met another woman. When he began to describe the relationship, I thought he would describe a purely sexual scenario in which a lonely older man finds a woman glad to be fussed over and showered with gifts. But the story evolved, just as their love affair had blossomed. "Repayment with gifts or money is never enough," Mr. P. said quietly. "I want to make her happy. I want to please her. I love this woman."

Discreetly and delicately, he described the sanctuary he shared with his lover. With great restraint he described the pattern of his escapes from his own guards, chauffeurs, and family that enabled him to be reunited with her again and again.

I grinned. "After all this time, why must you still sneak away in order to be with her? Surely, you have grieved long enough!"

His response held bitter words for his culture. Precautions were needed because the woman was from a lower caste. There would be extremely unfavorable consequences if it became known that Mr. P. were involved with someone regarded as beneath his status. "I know this seems strange to you in America, but it is of utmost importance in our society. For me, I am not concerned, however. It is for my children."

He kept his love secret because their liaison would have a profoundly negative effect upon the marriage prospects of his children. But now, even though his children were married, "I was struck by the potential fates of my grandchildren," he said. "Unfortunately, these societal views will not change so rapidly."

Now, due to his deteriorating health, he was confined to his house, and so his secret trips to his lover had come to an end. "I love her so much. She has been so good to me. Now I am dying. And I shall die without her. I will be alone."

I began to weep. He rose from his seat to embrace and console me. It pained me to imagine how this man I had grown to care for would miss his lover's embrace. I cried for his yearning to hear her voice or feel her touch at least once more. I cried for the dwindling days he had left on this earth. I thought of his longing for his love, and I wept.

He held my head to his chest and patted my shoulder. "I just needed you to know. I will die a lonely man … unwillingly. I am sorry, but I had to share this with you."

Years later, I still wonder how his story ended. I hope to God that he came to realize his life was more important than social mores, and that he and his lover followed their hearts to their true home.

Life lesson

Whenever I think of the power of leading from the heart, I'm reminded of these words from Eckhart Tolle, author of *The Power of Now* (Namaste Publishing):

> Most people do not know how to listen because the major part of their attention is taken up by thinking. They pay more attention to that than to what the other person is saying, and none at all to what really matters: the Being of the other person underneath the words and the mind. Of course, you cannot feel someone else's Being except through your own. This is the beginning of the realization

of oneness, which is love. At the deepest level of Being, you are one with all that is.

Most human relationships consist mainly of minds interacting with each other, not human beings communicating, being in communion. No relationship can thrive in that way, and that is why there is so much conflict in relationships. When the mind is running your life, conflict, strife and problems are inevitable. Being in touch with your inner body creates clear space of no-mind within which the relationship can flower.

How do you lead with your heart in your personal life? Try to be less calculating and analytical. Realize that if something is making you feel uncomfortable, there is a reason for your feeling, so trust your gut. Trust your emotions. Don't try to second-guess your heart. When you listen with your heart, you become nonjudgmental. When you listen with your mind, you judge. We can't help it. We're meaning-making machines.

Dr. Stephen Post, President of the Institute for Research on Unlimited Love at Case Western Reserve University School of Medicine, believes that happiness cannot be sought after or acquired. Instead, happiness results from doing good toward others. Happiness is the byproduct of such acts.

This reminds me of the interesting prescription Dr. Scott Bea has been giving his patients since long before the "positive psychology" movement became jargon in our profession. Bea advises depressed patients to find special things to give as gifts to others. One can appreciate the brilliance in such a simple task, where the focus is taken away from the negative-thinking mind and transferred to the actions of the hopeful heart.

The most intellectually gifted dancer cannot lead his partner effectively unless he uses his heart. Provocative words and thoughts will not move her. No matter how forceful, no amount of nudging, pushing, or pulling will bring about the desired dance move. Only through her partner's heart can she sense his purpose and intention. Only through his heart does he invite her to share his intention. This is the tango embrace.

If she's able to strengthen her form and quiet her mind, she'll be able to maintain her heart in front of his. And then they can carry out their shared intention, which, evolving, will transform them as they move to the music.

Chapter 6

Look into My Eyes, Not at My Feet

Here's a major difference between beginning dance students and those who are more advanced. Beginners try to learn techniques for leading by focusing on a teacher's feet. But the lead never comes from the feet or the legs. Dance steps are led from the chest – the heart, specifically – and sometimes the entire torso.

New students don't seem as interested in the parallel positioning of the chests and shoulders of the teacher and his partner. Often, students overlook the manner in which the follower receives her lead. They miss the receptiveness of her body, cradled confidently in the leader's embrace. In addition, the penetrating gaze of the teacher's eyes is discounted, as if they didn't consider it an important component of the step.

This reminds me of the first time I danced with Fred Holczer, an experienced Austrian dancer. I felt so self-conscious about my lack of experience that I watched our feet as we danced. From lack of confidence, I watched my feet, and from fear that he would step on me, I watched his. My fear greatly hindered both our interaction with the music and his ability to lead effectively.

One evening, while dancing at Sachsenheim's in Cleveland, Fred uttered a simple command in his charming Viennese accent. "Look into my eyes, don't look at your feet."

He led me into a series of *molinetes*, which required me to glide and pivot around my partner as he remained the axle of our wheel. As I kept my eyes on his, I noticed how my posture improved instantly, which permitted him a more effective lead. I was struck by the ease of our movements, which we executed without my watching our foot placements. But more important, by gazing into my partner's eyes, I could appreciate the source of the dance, which could only be seen through the eyes – the windows to the soul.

Arrogance is a two-way street

And now, here's a simple thought to live by. When you stop being self-conscious, you start being self-confident.

This lesson really hit home when I was in the third year of medical school. The third year includes medical students' first forays into hospitals and the real world of illness and pain. Everything we've learned in the classroom becomes so much more significant. The "practice" of medicine is not practice anymore. We're no longer reading about patients, we're trying to heal them.

In medical school, there's a phenomenon called "the imposter syndrome." Student doctors are so afflicted with self-doubt that they sit in class and think, "The people who run this program must've made a mistake when they accepted me. They couldn't have picked me to be a doctor; they must not have noticed that I don't fit in here." The imposter syndrome also flares up when you put on the white coat and patients start calling you doctor, when you're not even a licensed physician yet.

Interns who fall into the imposter syndrome are filled with self-doubt. Their fear keeps them from realizing their potential as healers. They may be gifted, intelligent, caring people whom the medical community would be proud to have in their ranks. Yet their fear holds them back. They look at their clipboards instead of into their patient's eyes, or they focus solely upon the disease, the wound, or the deformity, and not on the person.

Doctors stop feeling like imposters when they gain the confidence to look into the mirror and see a committed practitioner looking back at them.

The same is true for dancers.

I've come to realize that arrogance is a two-way street. It's illuminating to recognize that with our own confidence and maturity we encounter fewer arrogant people. Perhaps arrogance is simply the method insecure people use to interpret the world.

Overcoming shyness

In terms of dance, you must be as comfortable with your partner as you are with yourself.

Remember the "three-minute marriage"? Such "marriages" are made by couples who shed their inhibitions during the life of their dance and surrender themselves to the music and their partners. And afterward, if these people want to go back to being shy and reserved, very well. But credit them with the courage to open themselves up for three minutes and for daring to lose themselves in the mystery of the dance.

What I'm saying is that if you're too afraid to try, you'll never succeed as a dancer, because even before you step out onto the floor, you've already created in your mind a scenario of defeat.

Don't let shyness and self-consciousness defeat you. Try this. Think of the dance as a manufactured moment during which you can imagine yourself to be *anyone* you want. And tango can be fairly theatrical. This flamboyance seems to be allowed – even perhaps, encouraged.

And if you're worried because you're a beginner and don't have all the steps down, don't worry. In the first place, remember that all the dancers you see out on the floor began at one time by looking at their feet and practicing "one-two-three, one-two-three" with the teacher. Plus, many dancers are eager to help you. So have fun!

Here's how I helped my children beat shyness. Before they even started school, I taught them that when we had guests or when I was introducing them to someone, they had to extend a hand in friendship, look each person in the eye, and introduce themselves. I told my kids that shyness was no excuse for bad manners. There's something important about making eye contact. Looking someone in the eye tells that person that you're interested in him or her and that you have confidence in yourself.

And so it is with tango. Some partners dance close together because they enjoy looking into each other's eyes. Some women believe they can read a partner's choreography in his eyes. Others dance so close that their partners get blurry. I can't judge it – it works for them.

I believe you should dance just close enough that you can make eye contact with your partner and not feel intimidated. Some dancers call this "the piercing gaze." They dance without expression, but let their eyes do all the talking. Except me – I'm not a very dignified type. I crack up a lot when male dancers look at me with an oh-so-serious scowl. I've also been known to quote lines from movies like *Top Gun* while dancing. (Boy, do my dance partners have a terrific sense of humor.)

Life lesson

At times, we get too caught up in the footwork of life and forget to look into other people's eyes and smile. When you look at your feet, you become preoccupied with yourself. When you're looking at life – or into your partner's eyes – you're enriched by all the inevitable lessons that a journey provides.

Many years ago, a colleague told me about his grand plan to work in the field as a medical missionary. But first, of course, he dutifully listed everything he needed to do before he could begin, including pay off his debts, obtain funding, get to know lots of bigwigs who would back his plan, the works. I hate to make such a pessimistic prediction, but I'm almost certain he'll never end up actually pursuing medical missionary work. He's invented too many excuses for looking at his feet.

Coincidentally, within a few months of listening to that colleague's ambitions, I was invited by Dr. Jonathan Ross, a friend, to join his medical mission team to Guatemala. Inspired by his generosity and determination, I jumped at the offer. Later I accompanied him on several more missions. Despite his many professional and personal obligations, he committed himself to fulfilling his dream and achieving one of his purposes in life.

Leading from his heart, Dr. Ross began and has continued to nurture the progress of a little hospital in one of the poorest countries in Latin America. Though he's a disciplined and humble student of life in so many ways, he doesn't look at his feet while he's dancing. I've observed him with his family and his patients, and his focus is always on them.

My 88-year-old grandmother, to whom this book is dedicated, lives in her own little apartment in Mexico City. Though her home is modest, she has happily hosted countless parties featuring her famous cuisine. (Beware of people who can't invite you over until the remodeling is finished.) Even while she lived with me in Guanajuato, she never expressed any hesitation about moving, traveling, or entertaining. And we did much of this on a relatively large scale. Indeed, her focus was on relationships and on making people happy.

Incidentally, she was a fabulous dancer who, in her youth, cleared many ballroom floors in Mexico City with her dance partners. And, of course, she never looked at her feet.

Chapter 7

Grow with Each Step

"Grow with each step." Sounds like a Zen *koan*, doesn't it? Or maybe the author of this aphorism was a little confused – a dancer is supposed to *move* with each step, not grow. So what's with the phrase "grow with each step"?

Tango teacher Timmy Tango explained it this way. "Straighten your legs. Take longer strides." Tioma, another teacher, said, "Be like a spring – tall when you complete the step." Okay, makes sense. But Mario, my teacher in Buenos Aires, put it in perspective. Under his tutelage, I began to expand my chest with deep inbreaths at the end of every one or two measures of music. Practicing this simple motion, I began sensing my growth as a dancer.

To grow with each step, maintain your height and posture so that your axis is always vertical and strong. Sometimes that can hurt. But when you become accustomed to standing with a good posture, you'll be able to recognize how unbalanced you feel when you're not standing tall. We may feel comfortable when we're crouched down or hidden, but as we learn to walk properly, we realize that we actually gain more balance and strength from our growth. And once you experience that sense of height and powerful chest expansion, and that nice lengthening of the ventrum, you'll recognize that your balance has also been enhanced.

For me, growing also meant conquering one of my biggest challenges, dancing with men who aren't as tall as I am. I'm 5-foot-8; in heels, I can grow to 5-11 or 6 feet. Sometimes I dance with men who are 5-foot-5 or even shorter. Nowadays, I *never* dance in a slouch or crouch, but I used to. Believe it or not, I used to slouch and hunch my back when I danced with shorter men. Now, when my partner is much shorter, I become especially aware of my balance. If my weight-bearing leg is slightly bent in an effort to expose my ventrum for the lead, my non-weight-bearing leg maintains the show of elegance by being straight. I do this by accentuating a "pretty foot." (I'll explain this term shortly.)

In a literal sense, "grow with each step" means to make the stride longer and the chest cavity larger by standing straighter because we have a tendency to shrink a bit as the dance goes on. Or if the dancer feels a tad intimidated or insecure, the challenge is to remain tall.

There's a metaphorical lesson here, too. "Growing" means broadening your knowledge and trying new things. It's very challenging to try something new when you're feeling insecure, because you're exposing yourself to the unknown. But that's the only way growth can happen.

Don't compromise your height

I often feel uncomfortable when my partner is a head shorter than I am. In a close embrace, he'd be smothered between my breasts. So we dance in a different style. But I've taken dance classes with several teachers who are on the shorter side and within thirty seconds, I no longer notice our height difference. In fact, I feel fabulous with them.

In the past when I danced with shorter partners, I wasn't aware that my body gradually recoiled from them as the dance went on. My strides shortened and my posture worsened as I bent my back to meet them. These movements on my part undoubtedly reflected a lifelong self-consciousness about being taller than all the boys in my class. Not only that, I was grossly skinny and covered with acne. I'm sure that my past was haunting me.

My dance teachers began pointing out what I was doing and suggested that I try to be mindful of holding my height throughout the dance. Once, one of my teachers even said, "Stop being so scared." *How can I stop being scared?* I wondered. Then, through experimentation, I realized that the key to keeping my posture and strength was through my breathing. (It also helped to remind myself that I hadn't been a teenager for *decades*.)

A milestone came when I was dancing with my teacher Mario in Buenos Aires. He not only showed me that taking deep breaths helped me remember to stay straight, he made me breathe along with the measures of the music. Now, I'm no longer conscious of my breathing. And my dance steps flow.

For a tall female dancer, feeling good means maintaining the axis and not stooping to anyone. You know your abilities, and when you're with someone who knows how to lead, his height isn't a handicap. When I'm dancing with some men who are shorter than I am, I have an absolute blast. It's as if their confidence makes them grow with each step.

"Pretty foot"

A "pretty foot" uses the ball of the foot to make "drawings" on the floor. Each drawing (*lapis*) should be done with this portion of the foot while three to four inches of your heel maintains contact against the floor, somewhat like a rudder. The aesthetics of this maneuver are delicious.

Another pretty foot movement involves the pointed toe. It's a rule in tango that if the foot leaves the floor, the toes must be pointed – that is, unless small walking embellishments are being performed. Sometimes such steps require an exaggerated dorsiflexion of the foot.

Don't try to draw attention to yourself when you're making a pretty foot. It's not something to be performed hastily or carelessly. The pretty foot is a very thoughtful movement. You're executing the maneuver to maintain the aesthetics of the dance. You can also use it to compensate for great disparities in height by bending one knee and keeping the other straight, but extended. By making the "pretty foot" on the extended, non-weight-bearing side, you can keep your balance and still complement your partner's height.

Growing as a physician

I grew as a doctor when, in the mid-1990s, I took some long steps and began prescribing some unconventional therapies for patients who were diagnosed with chronic prostatitis/pelvic-pain syndrome. Though many of these "unconventional" therapies have now become accepted in the mainstream medical community, back then I was a bit of a rebel for prescribing exercise, physical therapy, myofascial trigger-point release, stress management, relaxation techniques, and sometimes psychological counseling accompanied by biofeedback. I have to admit, at the time I was nervous about what I was doing. *Am I really helping my patients*, I wondered fretfully, *or am I just giving them false hope?*

Let me tell you, I felt as if I were standing on some very scary ground. I was treating patients completely differently from what had been the standard for decades – and from what I had been taught to do during four years of medical school (and another four years of residency). For example, I wasn't prescribing antibiotics for men who had a supposed infection of the prostate gland or prostatitis. I didn't put them through a gauntlet of urological tests or perform invasive procedures for patients who had so-called urological complaints. Yet people weren't getting worse, they were getting better. And they were coming back to me. This nurtured my confidence, and I think my patients felt it.

Yes, I was an all-important doctor in a white coat now, but before I entered medical school, I was an "Earth mother/ granola chick" looking for some credibility. I wanted to practice medicine in a natural and holistic manner. So I began to do a lot more hand-holding and listening. And that's when it occurred to me, *Wow, that's why I went into medicine!* Yet I was afraid of growing away from conventional medicine. While the white coat and my prescription pad may have given me an appearance of authority, inside I felt that I wasn't standing tall and confidently recommending these new therapies that I, in my heart, believed in.

So I did a little research. When I questioned my patients I found that more than 75 percent of the ones who had embraced my suggestions were reporting significant improvement or complete resolution of their symptoms. Though I was still curious about why this was happening, I concluded that their taking my advice was a positive prognostic sign. In other words, a patient's chances of improving were directly linked with his willingness to keep his appointments with me.

Two years later, I found that the compliance rate had increased dramatically. Nearly all my patients kept their appointments, with many of them traveling up to five hours by car, several times per month. Some even arrived by plane. Nothing had really changed in terms of my patient demographics. The only plausible variables had to be me and the manner in which I engaged my patients.

One day, I was explaining my unconventional approach to a patient when I noticed how impassioned I was as I told him about holistic therapies and how empowering they are. It dawned on me that my patients' desire to improve was because of *me*. Even though I may have felt timid earlier in my career about suggesting unconventional approaches, I *knew* deep down that these therapies were safe and effective. And as results accumulated over the years, my confidence and passion had grown. My patients must have picked up on my burgeoning faith – their belief in me became the first step in their healing therapy. This gave me more confidence that I was doing the right thing.

My growth as a listener and healer fortified my effectiveness. I grew in my quest to be authentic and genuine. This translated into an even higher compliance rate among my patients, who became able to begin the challenging regimen of daily self-care. They, too, went from self-conscious to self-confident.

The importance of elegance

There's another aspect to the concept of growing with each step. It turns out that confidence is as much about the way we present ourselves as it is about what we're feeling inside. Acting *as if* we feel strong and assured actually helps us become that way.

In dance, for example, movement should never look as if it's a struggle. It should never seem as if an inordinate amount of exertion is involved. Faced with an obstacle, then, how do you overcome it?

Try this on for size. No matter the cost, in life, as in dance, never sacrifice elegance.

It took me many lessons and several teachers to learn how to grow with each step. I'd practice and practice and then go back and learn more. Eventually I got it. Some people, though, refuse to realize that you grow through learning. Or they get discouraged because they don't "get it" on the first try. They give up too easily and miss out on great opportunities for growth.

I used to notice how frustrated some people became when they couldn't figure out their career path or find a way to achieve a goal. They often missed out on other opportunities because they couldn't see a purpose in learning a task. I discovered that it's the people who don't give up who end up taking longer and longer strides. They're the ones who end up being able to lead and then take their dance to the next level.

Every experience, class, or job provides useful lessons. You might not appreciate them fully at the time, but these building blocks, especially if they're extremely different, provide a broad base to your foundation. We construct our lives out of so many disparate parts that sometimes it seems as if it takes a long time for our lives to come together. But all the time, we're building.

I often think of an analogy that came to me back in college. When I was younger, it seemed that many people around me were soaring atop their constructions, which I imagined as tall, thin, pointed structures like the Washington Monument. Then I realized that I was building a pyramid. And many years later, I can say that despite its shorter stature, the pyramid is firm and stable. It can't be toppled like those dazzling but precarious structures that grew too tall, too quickly.

Our journey of life contains many steps, and we need to master each one along the way. Hardship or a timid nature can cause us to contract or shrink with each step, which limits our repertoire of moves. It can also limit our views of people, relationships, and destiny.

The wise individual uses hardship to grow. Discomfort is the incentive that forces us to strengthen the muscles of our emotions, intellect, and soul. (That's why it's called "growing pains.") If things come too easily or the way is too smooth, we aren't challenged to stretch ourselves – and we don't grow.

In dance, as with any exercise, we have to keep our stubborn hamstrings elastic. They may hurt as we lengthen them, but the resulting beauty, agility, and strength enables us to perform our tasks with elegance and grace.

GLOSSARY

Dorsiflexion: A turning-up of the foot or toes.

A fluid embrace flows from sensitivity and trust (left).

They respond best who anticipate least (above).

Dr. Potts' partner: Jorge Niedas. Photos by Steve Travarca.

A basic sidestep can be a bridge, a balance point, or a building block (left).

It takes two to tango:
The partners are equally
accountable (left).

The best lead is a
shared intention
(above).

Talk distracts.
The steps speak for
themselves (left).

Watch the eyes, not the feet (right).

A strong vertical axis lends courage to try new things (below).

False steps are impossible when you lead from the heart (below).

A stolen lead can be an elegant secret joke (left).

When you're centered, you can defy gravity (right).

"My partner transferred his weight from one foot to the other so gently, it felt as if he were taking a breath" (left).

Chapter 8

Express Yourself: Interlead

Interleading is a form of tango. It represents an intimate dialogue between the dance partners, and it's a little mischievous. In interleading, the woman steals the lead from the man, but does it discreetly because the act is not supposed to be obvious to onlookers. An interlead involves just a movement or two and lasts only a few seconds. Supposedly, interleading isn't allowed in places like Argentina, where dance purists consider it heresy.

I learned about it from Virginia Kelly at Dance Manhattan in New York City, where the women in the class were instructed to steal the leads from the men as we alternated dance partners. "It shouldn't be obvious to onlookers, but you have to get the guy's attention so you can take the lead," said Virginia.

While the interlead requires neither strength nor aggression (in fact, those two qualities undermine it), it does require me to show an extra level of attentiveness to my partner. Not only do I have to listen to his lead with my body, but I have to pay attention to his weight transfer so that I can plan my takeover strategy. I have to be extremely sensitive in order to execute this maneuver because if I interject my move imprecisely, I can throw off his balance and even injure him.

My growing sensitivity to my partner's position and balance made me more appreciative of the fine leading men with whom I have danced. The best ones never coerced the dance step, and they have selflessly showcased my strength as a follower.

Virginia went on to caution the women in class about the risk we'd be taking, since there are many men "who would not appreciate or feel comfortable with such play." The implications of her statement seem familiar in the context of human relationships. How well can men handle such brazen self-expression? Which men will celebrate their partners' creativity and playfulness? And what kind of leader would be strong and confident enough to relinquish his control with dignity and agility?

It makes for a subtle paradox. In interleading, I have to be sensitive enough to steal my partner's lead, and he has to be strong enough to enjoy my audacity. I can't use force to steal his lead or to get his attention. To the contrary, I have to be as sensitive and conscious of his balance as he is of mine, so that when I seize my opportunity, it will be something that he'll enjoy too.

In addition, interleading can't be something that just makes me look good. I have to do for my partner what he does for me – I must make the maneuver look like something that he, too, would be proud to incorporate into the dance.

One more word on interleading. It shouldn't be confused with back-leading, where the woman is leading and being rigid, or trying to put herself into the man's lead. There's no excuse for such a move. It makes a woman into a partner who is stubborn and heavy, rather than graceful and lightfooted.

A sense of give and take

As I realized my importance in interleading, I began to wonder, *What kinds of thoughts run through the minds of our male dance partners?*

A wimpy guy won't let a woman take over. If I interlead, I'm going to be presenting my partner with a new step that he wasn't prepared for, and then he'll have to pick up the lead from that spot. To enjoy interleading, a man has to be strong enough to withstand the sudden turning of the tables and to be able to take over from there.

How will he know you've taken the lead from him? You could preempt the move by being playful – doing a lot of unexpected little things like tapping the foot or taking a little longer with an embellishment (I'll explain this in a moment) to signal that you're not going to do the typical thing or that you're not a typical woman. This alerts him to the fact that he has to be on his toes.

With some steps you know that if he's going in a certain direction, you can say to yourself, *A-ha! If he's going to do such-and-such, I can quickly hook my leg around him because he's not going to be on that weight-bearing leg. Or I can swipe his foot out from under him because I know his weight is transferring to the other leg.* It's the same as if you were playing with anyone. But you have to have a sense of whether your partner will be open to that kind of play. Some men don't enjoy that sort of give-and-take.

An embellishment is an extra little move that you add to a regular step. I have a great repertoire of them. For example, if a man puts me in a *parada* – a stop – and invites me to walk over his leg, I could simply walk over his leg, or I could shine my shoe on his leg before I walk over it. I could give myself a shoeshine, or I could tap my foot up his calf to the rhythm of the music. I could also hesitate, make *lapises* (drawings) on the floor with my foot, and keep the dance in suspense. And sometimes, when he puts my foot in a sandwich (he crisscrosses his feet and sandwiches my foot between his), I will sandwich him, too, doing the same thing back, which sometimes he doesn't expect.

Interleading is like a little game. When I took an interleading class, I danced with a lesbian dancer, which was perfect, because she was already used to leading. We became very playful during class, exchanging the lead after every few dance steps. When there was a great pause in the music, the follower tried to get the leader into another kind of move. I called it a little tango chess game.

Some men don't like to give up the lead

Luckily, I haven't encountered a man who didn't want to give up the lead. Then again, I've rarely played the interleading game outside New York, and I've executed the move with very few people. In part it's my lack of experience and in part a sixth sense about the person I'm dancing with, since as I said, some men find interleading uncomfortable.

Why are some leaders like that? When I feel that a man won't yield at all – well, if he's a good lead and I enjoy dancing with him – I'll always let him lead. I may think to myself, *This is how the dance works for him, so I have to enjoy this dance the way he wants to do it.* I may feel sorry for him, because he doesn't want to try anything new, but I won't feel rejected. You can't take something like this personally.

The other side of the coin is that when you steal the lead, you don't want to treat the man as if you're disregarding him as a partner.

Let me explain what I mean. Sometimes I run into a man who feels so technically advanced that he can't wait to show the world how many moves he knows. This kind of man has no respect for women.

For a man like this, I become an ornament. I dance as if I'm his showpiece. He flings me around until I feel as if we're going through a wrestling match. Afterward, I feel as if I've been nothing more than a prop he used to show off his prowess. Used, in fact, is the operative word.

So when a woman, by the same token, is trying to scheme her little leads, she should see to it that her partner doesn't feel misused or abused. Stealing the lead should be something so subtle that he ends up smiling, as if the interlead act is the couple's personal joke that no one else knows about.

Off the dance floor, I cringe when women overtly or vulgarly "steal leads" for the sake of equality. Such manipulative behavior shows little respect for men. Stealing the lead in tango isn't some sort of ballbusting feminist gesture. Mutual respect, I believe, is the main ingredient.

This reminds me of the proverbial story cited in the book *Getting to Yes*, by Roger Fisher, Bruce M. Patton, and William L. Ury, which illustrates the importance of communication and the spirit of sharing in healthy negotiation. In this story, two children are fighting over a single remaining orange. A "wise" mediator cuts the orange precisely in half. Dispute resolved, right? Wrong.

Later, it is discovered that half an intact orange peel has been thrown into the rubbish, while half the juicy fruit was discarded into yet another wastebasket. The result of such narrow-mindedness? The waste of half the orange.

So often we get caught up in obtaining "our fair share," becoming obsessed with entitlement and the pursuit of "equality." I discovered that tango offers me complete fulfill-ment because I bring 100 percent of my femininity to the dance. There is no need for "analysis" that would thwart my role or purpose. When I dance I'm being completely true to my nature.

Dance, to me, is about recognizing who I am and what I need. (Most human beings, by the way, want far more than they need.) Sometimes I need the protective, spicy peel and sometimes I need the refreshing inner fruit. This is true of loving relationships in which people can dance together without keeping score or taking inventory. When you become secure in the person you are, you can no longer feel demeaned. Indeed, at times you can take quiet pride in your ability to be submissive or subservient when such virtues are called upon. When you dance in this manner, you begin to realize that the orange is much more fragrant and juicy. Relationships broaden and that which is shared can become limitless.

Interleading in life

Interleading becomes most intriguing to me when I reflect on my role as a doctor. On the dance floor, I can playfully steal the lead from the man. As a physician whose patients are all men, I am the healer and must take the lead. Sometimes, though, I allow my patients to steal the lead from me.

One of my patients is also a very successful business owner. Over the course of several years I have come to understand both his sensitive insights and his no-nonsense approach to life. One afternoon, he revealed sudden changes in his symptoms that warranted additional testing he absolutely wished to avoid. "Especially that cystoscopy," he grumbled, rolling his eyes. "That tube going up my urethra. Sheesh." Yet by the end of our appointment, we had set up not only a CT scan, but also the dreaded cystoscopy. On the way to the scheduler's office, we were exchanging anecdotes about travel and child-rearing when suddenly he turned and asked, "How'd you do that?"

"Do what?" I asked.

"How'd you get me to agree to go through with those tests?"

"Interleading," I replied with a chuckle. "It's when a female tango dancer respectfully steals the lead from her dance partner."

I had not frightened or coerced my patient into having the procedures done. I acknowledged his apprehensions and he honored me with his trust. This trust enables our patients to allow us to perform invasive diagnostic tests in their genital regions.

After nearly thirteen years in urology, I remain impressed by men who are willing to be open-minded about having a female doctor. For example, the stereotype that Muslim men will not let a woman touch them in their private places is incorrect. I learned this over a decade ago from an Iranian patient and his son, who accompanied him as translator.

At the time, I had only been in practice for a few months and assumed that being a woman would offend men seeking urological care. I apologized to every man who walked into my office.

"I'm so sorry, I know you thought you'd be seeing a man, and I hope I'm not making you more uncomfortable." I had my little speech down pat.

I was sure that this Iranian man, a Muslim, would be startled to learn that I was his physician. I began our examination with an apology, which the son translated rather quickly. I sat quietly, glancing at them occasionally, waiting about the older man's reaction.

To my surprise, sharp wrinkles appeared at the corners of his eyes. The two exchanged a few more words and chuckles. I felt myself blushing. The younger man turned from his father to face me and with the most charming expression, translated his father's response. "My father," he said slowly, "has … noooooooooo … problem seeing you." The older man nodded as he gave me a sweet, paternal smile. And that was the last time I ever apologized to any patient for being a woman.

Here's why I find it so easy to treat men. I let them be men. I'm never taken aback by someone opening the door for me, calling me "honey," or complimenting or flirting with me. None of that fazes me. They're just being themselves. I navigate it and get them to do what they need to do. That's the simple part. The complicated part comes when I have to ask some tough questions. Why aren't you taking better care of yourself? Why do you feel unfulfilled? Why are you unhappy?

Men talk about things with me that they'd never talk about with their wives. This is especially true in terms of sexuality. I think it's because they're in a medical setting and talking with someone who's not threatening. Ironically, it's a lot easier for them to talk about impotence to a woman than it would be to another man.

My patients are so practical, straightforward, and candid. When you ask them a question, they're right there.

I once asked a 75-year-old farmer, "How's your love life?" and he said, "I make love to the wife twice a month. Wish it was four times a month, but it's twice a month. And, Dr. Potts, I do a good job and I don't need any of the Viagra." And then he told me what sexual practices he and his wife were and were not into. Yikes! My patients are never ashamed to tell me anything. But sometimes they tell me too much.

I think male depression is so misunderstood. Men have many creative ways to disguise depression, and I don't think they'll start taking better care of themselves unless they first feel good about themselves. Because men feel vulnerable when it comes to their health, they find it less threatening for a woman to tell them how to take care of themselves. It plants the seeds of curiosity about what's sabotaging their therapy and their health.

The follower as leader

My dance teacher Mario once told me, "Don't ever dance for a man." What he was saying was "Make the man dance for you. Not the other way around." He was very emphatic about that.

This is the undercurrent of interleading. If you, as a woman, as a follower, do the step the way he wants it done, but you're not letting him lead it, then you make it easy for him not to dance for you. When he doesn't dance for you, he's not elevating the dance. That means that you – as the follower – can elevate the dance to a higher level by demanding that he punch up the lead. *Don't get sloppy with me*, is your unspoken message. *Be precise!*

That was a valuable lesson. During one exercise in which we were dancing in circles, Mario kept asking, "Why are you going around? Why are you syncopating?"

"Because that's the way the step is," I answered.

He said, "I didn't lead it that way."

"But I was taught that doing this step means going on your back to get syncopated."

"No, the man has to lead that syncopation. It's a solid step-step-step-step."

Again I begged to differ. "Men don't do that."

He looked at me sternly. "Well, you're responsible for making that man lead. If he doesn't lead, you have to do the step the way he's led it; in fact, if he leads it without the syncopation, you do it without the syncopation. The fact that you let him get away with that makes you an accomplice and makes you a bad dancer." *Ouch!*

Tango is a dialogue between two people, and interleading takes that conversation to a more daring level. Don't let yourself feel powerless because you're following someone else's lead. Questioning the lead or even seizing it for a short time doesn't mean that you're trying to undermine the leader or be rebellious.

One goal of dance is to make your partner better. You're helping that person grow. So interleading can serve a valuable function. You're telling the leader that you're not going to let him get away with half-assed leads. Just remember, interleading requires a great deal of sensitivity. Not force.

Chapter 9

Follow What You Lead

The leader is aware of his partner's strengths and limitations as he guides her through the steps he has imagined for them. At times, he'll pivot to lead her, and she may take numerous side-to-side steps around him. He makes sure that she follows through on each step he has asked her to take and waits before he asks her to do more.

This shows the mark of a good leader. He's clear about conveying "orders" and is conscientious about the welfare of his partner. He invites her to share his intention and respects her ability to complete the interpretation.

One of my favorite partners, Jorge Niedas, a former ballet dancer in Argentina, takes the art of waiting to the ultimate level. Not only does he pause like a beautiful statue, waiting for me to complete my embellishments, but he also waits for me to reorient myself into his embrace. These are indeed the most subtle and yet most voluptuous pauses I've experienced in tango. I sigh, remembering them.

Mario, my teacher in Buenos Aires, made me feel comfortable from the first moment of our first dance. I knew immediately that he had sensed all my strengths and – alas – weaknesses. Yet he never made me feel self-conscious in any way. By the time we were engaged in our second dance, he had kicked my feet out from under me numerous times, bringing me to lunges, dips, and other positions I'd never imagined I could execute. I stole glimpses in the studio's mirrors and admired the tableaux of lovely lines made effortlessly by his masculine lead and my unhesitating ability to follow him everywhere.

Our dances were wonderful experiences because as leader, he made me feel safe. His lessons were supportive, nurturing, and validating. I was confident that he'd never allow me to fall, slip, or even stub my little toe. My dancing improved dramatically after my short visit to Buenos Aires. Later, Mario remarked, "You must be very good, to allow me to forget I am your teacher." Wow. Such a good leader, and so gracious, too.

A year later we performed together as invited guests at a prestigious national surgical convention in Mexico.

The audience loved us, and people thought we made a wonderful team.

Now, years later, I still think about Mario's qualities as a leading man. What was it about him that fostered such immediate closeness and comfort?

The shared intention

A good leader is a good communicator and a good planner. He must imagine the steps leading to the next move and know how to begin that maneuver while his partner may not be finished with the last move. Starting a new move too early could result in the partner feeling rushed and even harmed. A leader who does this is obviously not listening to his partner's movements, nor has he been mindful of the steps he initiated and requested. So a good leader must show empathy for those he is leading.

People who have been in the trenches, so to speak, are generally better leaders. They also tend to be better listeners and to convey the lead well. I suppose it's credibility that they possess. They're confident in what they do, and because they know their partner's attributes they're adept at refining the lead as the dance continues. After all, the lead is never static; it evolves in a melding of the leader's expectations and the follower's skills.

That's why the embrace in tango is called the shared intention, because the leader has invited his partner to share the intention of the dance with him. The intention, of course, is to create an experience that both partners find enjoyable. And perhaps the leader will also teach the follower something about the dance. Who knows? Perhaps the follower will teach the leader a thing or two.

You know, the lay press and the media are replete with information about leadership, and yet most of us, most of the time, are followers. I think it's important to see the strength and power in following. The less talked-about and perhaps the more humble part of the partnership or team is the follower. Yet the one who follows has a role of great significance, and when we're following we should be aware of everything our job entails.

There's wisdom in following. After all, we make choices about the person we entrust with leading. We don't anticipate, we prepare, so that we're able to explore new patterns in the dance. If we slip into anticipating, we can stagnate any process or relationship. So we, too, must be accountable. Our ability to trust and be led is an indication of our strength, not our weakness. And as I mentioned in the previous chapter, by helping our leader grow, we can elevate the dance.

Indeed, as followers, we have an obligation to make leaders aware, to make *them* follow what they lead. (Parents of teenagers can testify that adolescents are innately skilled in this area.)

The same is true in corporate situations. A leader must be able to communicate his expectations while taking his followers' abilities into consideration. The leader must be open to feedback in order to ensure that he's conveying his lead appropriately and that others are provided with resources or time to carry out the company mission.

We've all known leaders so impressive that they inspired us to share their goals. Working with them became a learning experience – and that was exactly each leader's plan! When a leader creates a shared intention, followers develop confidence in the mission, their leader, and themselves. They feel supported, and their level of performance rises. In the end, everyone shares the credit for a job well done.

Creative visualization

Tango leaders practice creative visualization. When they're confident in their ability to initiate and perform a maneuver, they imagine how they can help their partner make the dance lovely – and within a fraction of a second, they manifest that movement and create it with their partner.

Athletes do something similar when they train for a big event. Marathon runners, for example, as part of their training, will picture themselves hitting the ribbon and breaking through the finish line.

As a tango dancer, I don't visualize the steps because I feel as if then I'd be anticipating. But I do prepare myself. I imagine a sensation beyond the visual, in which I just *know* that my maneuvers will be pretty and that I will be satisfied, and I *feel* myself being proud to have shared or experienced my abilities. Maybe I should call this an emotional visualization. It is a form of creative visualization, although I don't see an image. But I do feel what I expect and hope will occur.

Dancing with myself

It would be wrong to assume that the leader is not following at times. His partner may have a different mood, a different reaction time, or a different body type, all of which contribute to her unique interpretation of his lead. In order to understand how he can lead her, he has to attempt several different moves.

Similarly, I've danced with leaders who tried deep lunges in spite of having just met me. They ended up throwing my weight off and leaving me suspended. Some of these guys are really into acrobatics, but some of them can be fun. To these leaders, tango is "an extreme contact sport," as Dr. Neil Garbutt, a dear friend, once put it.

I've been asked how one becomes comfortable with that kind of leader. First, I answer, you must become comfortable with yourself.

I found that my dancing ability improved when I practiced alone. At first it's very difficult to practice by yourself. You quickly realize how much you've been relying on another person for balance. So the first thing you must do is gradually build up your core muscle strength.

Athletic trainers would be horrified to see how I work out because I'm either barefoot or in high-heeled shoes. I lift weights barefoot and frequently carry 10- to 15-pound dumbbells in each hand as I dance in my high heels. I do a lot of back steps and make my stride wider and wider.

Holding the weights, I work on building core strength by lifting my legs one at a time while balancing one leg with the heel. And then I do forward and backward *ochos* with the pivot, which is very difficult to do without holding onto someone, and I perform *molinetes* by going around in a circle on both sides. I do it that way to be prepared for partners who might be stronger on one side than the other.

I recommend these exercises for everyone. I once told the wife of Timmy Progros, one of my teachers, that we don't get enough chances to practice because we don't have enough tango venues in Cleveland. She said, "What does that have to do with anything?" Joanne made me realize that there's no excuse for not being able to practice, even if you must practice alone.

Janet Sutta, a tango dancer in New York City, said, "If you can't do a whole performance by yourself, then you can't tango."

As I said previously, I also practice my skills through creative visualization. Even though most of my practicing alone has been as a follower, I have practiced leading. When I picture myself leading, I imagine how I'm moving. In my mind's eye I see everything that's going to be involved for the follower to execute.

It's really worthwhile to practice alone and imagine how your partner is going to carry out everything that you expect. It helps you take what you know to the next level. And you also then appreciate the types of obstacles you may encounter on the way as well as what you need to do to either mitigate each challenge or create learning opportunities for your partners. Hence, leaders must follow their own leads, or else the step – the mission or the lesson – will never be brought to completion.

In addition, when you practice alone, you have moments of introspection where you realize your strengths and weaknesses. This is very important – you don't want to lead past the point of your own skill or knowledge. If you're not familiar with your capabilities, you could make your partner look awkward or injure your partner or yourself. It takes conscientious preparation to create an effective dance.

Being asked to lead or being offered a promotion, for example, can be very seductive. However, we must be humble enough to know when a leadership role may exceed our ability. We can't allow a prestigious title to distract us from the responsibilities involved. If we don't know what we're getting ourselves and others into, it can be disastrous for all.

Manifesting love

What works in dance works in all relationships. Just as exercising by yourself builds muscle strength, learning to enjoy your own company builds your inner strength. You can't lead or be led by someone else if you're not comfortable with yourself.

When you're happy with yourself, you're dancing for pleasure – your own and that of your partner. But when you're dancing purely to be admired by another person, you're dancing without love. That dance is destructive because you're seeking something that you don't possess: respect. And how can you demand respect from others if you don't feel it in yourself?

Love is a reflection of yourself; when you love yourself, you want to make yourself better for yourself and for the other person. In *The Road Less Traveled*, M. Scott Peck defined love as the "will to extend one's self for the purpose of nurturing one's own or another's spiritual growth." How true. Love comes from the impulse to make another person happy.

You're not going to be able to lead people effectively if you don't take all their steps into account. That means helping them to do better or to take better care of themselves. You can't impose on people what you want them to do. You can't threaten or penalize them.

In dance, in medicine, and in life, the key is to find out why people don't want to take better care of themselves. What's going on at home, what's affecting their self-esteem? Do they feel valued and worthy? People who feel unworthy or unvalued don't take good care of themselves. People who have deep-seated problems or unhappiness don't change until they find motivation.

Sometimes I think of the adage "when the student is ready, the teacher appears." People won't change their lives, try an exercise program, change a relationship, or begin to love themselves if they're not ready.

Dr. Mansour, a leader

I'm going to leave the dancing stage for a few moments to tell you about one of the finest leaders I've ever met. During my third year of medical school, I became interested in urology and asked some urologists about career possibilities. They laughed at me and told me I wouldn't have any customers.

At the time, I thought, *Oh, they're just being kind and looking out for me.* In retrospect, I think they were jerks.

But I really liked the field. I was attracted to things that were very private, very intimate. I felt comfortable in urology, not squeamish. I also loved surgery – I loved working with my hands. I liked how physical it was. I liked the immediate results of surgery, the artistry. In medicine, there's something very powerful about a person who can change things so dramatically.

And then I met one of my mentors. As a medical student in surgery, I came to treasure the chief of surgery at Cleveland's MetroHealth Medical Center, Dr. Edward Mansour. He asked medical students to work right beside him. He always clamped the edge of the surgical drape to his gown and put his tools there, so he didn't ask the nurse to pass him his instruments. Once, when he opened up an abdomen to hunt for an incidental tumor, he said to me, "Give me your hands." He took both my hands and we explored the patient's body together. He asked me to describe everything in the body I was touching and what I thought it was.

The inside of the body is very sensuous. The body cavity is so nice and warm that you want to keep your hands in there. (This is especially true for me since the surgical suites are usually chilly and I have Raynaud's Disease, a condition that makes some areas of my body feel numb and cool.)

I felt the rhythmic pulsation of the aorta, the muscular diaphragm going up and down, the diffuse sponginess of the liver. And I ran the bowel, going through the intestines with their balloonlike skin, making sure everything was okay. The way the bowel fans out from the lacy mesentery is very pretty. You can lift it up and look at it.

I remember being so afraid that I would break a blood vessel if I touched something too suddenly. Intellectually I knew this wouldn't happen, but I touched the organs with the utmost delicacy nonetheless. I was so careful with my hands.

I don't know whether everyone has had that kind of beautiful experience in surgery. I was so lucky to have Dr. Mansour leading me that day.

Practicing encouragement

Like Dr. Mansour, Mario was a perfect leader. It was an unforgettable experience to perform a successful dance with an expert partner who realized my strengths and shortcomings, and made me feel uninhibited and safe. He respected and nurtured me; I knew that he would never scold, humiliate, or injure me. Imagine being able to receive such trust from our employers, friends, and life partners.

I always share the story of Mario when I lead sensitivity-training workshops, because I know that the leaders in the audience (especially those who are men) would appreciate having someone describe them in such a trusting and appreciative way. If you or I were in the role of leader, we'd love to know that the people we work with are giving us that kind of recognition or telling other people that "my partner makes me feel so comfortable" or "that person makes me feel valued, and I can honestly say that when I dance with this leader, I really feel that I'm giving the best dance I can. I go beyond even my own expectations and beyond my limitations." How wonderful to know that people trust you so much that they surrender to you.

That should always be our goal.

A leader leads by encouraging others. "Follow what you lead" is an invitation to encourage more mindfulness in yourself along with more awareness of what you expect from others.

Every time the thought of encouragement comes to mind, I remember that its root word is "courage." And did you know that the root word for courage is "heart"?

Chapter 10

Dance More, Talk Less

When I'm being led, nothing annoys me more than when my partner keeps talking into my ear. And it's even more annoying if this one-sided conversation consists of nothing but orders and commands about what to do and when to do it. I'd rather just be led into executing a step, not lectured at as if this were the first time I'd ever worn dance shoes.

The biggest culprits behind this behavior are men who think they're better dancers than their partners and who therefore misinterpret any inability to execute a dance step as an inability to follow a lead. But leaders who are sensitive – *ah!* I can't find the words to describe the exhilaration of dancing with a stranger who leads so beautifully that he's able to entice me into more and more complicated moves with each musical measure – and who completes the most delicious of *tandas* without ever uttering a word!

Delightful leaders come in different styles. There are the ones who simply navigate me back to the starting point to repeat the lead, coaxing delicately and mindfully until I grasp their choreography. From there, we continue in silence, enjoying the music and perhaps a mutual smile. These leaders I treasure – the "strong, silent types."

I've danced with masters. They don't speak. They smile. Silence is indeed golden.

Talking, talking, talking

Why do some leaders feel that they need to keep reminding you who's in charge? Perhaps these dance-floor microman-agers don't trust their followers. Being directed with harshly spoken words instead of being guided by movement is very demeaning. It means that the leader is assuming that his partner doesn't know anything. And then the follower feels insulted because she's not being listened to.

If the leader has a clear objective of what he wants the dance to accomplish, and if he carries out his lead properly, he doesn't need to lecture his partner. Unless you're in a class setting, you don't want lessons on the dance floor. It's so rude to hear from a leader, "I want you to move over here. This is what *I'm* doing and you're *not* doing. Move over here when I get ready." Well, you know what? That leader's body language wasn't inviting me to go in the direction he's dreaming about – that's why I didn't go there. His movements didn't lead me there.

Here's faux pas No. 2. After the dance, the insecure leader feels as if he must dissect the follower's flaws and prove why he wasn't at fault when a maneuver wasn't executed perfectly. Good leaders don't need to hold post-dance discussions to analyze every move. An effective leader has no reason to explain, excuse, or rationalize. If he steps on your toe once and apologizes, that's fine, but if every little thing ends up as an apology, he has no business leading.

Too much discussion, to me, means too little preparedness and too little self-assurance.

I'm not saying you should *never* talk. Honest observations are good. Feedback will help you become a better dancer. But ask for feedback first. In fact, before the dance begins, you may want to ask your leader if he'd like to share any observations afterward.

Then again, some leaders don't want to be instructors – they just want to dance, get the job done, and move on to another partner. And still others get a perverse pleasure out of giving and/or receiving negative feedback. Every now and again, someone will come along to rain on your parade, and you'll just have to open your umbrella and endure the downpour.

To actually seek conversation, however, is like looking for trouble. That's why I'd rather be dancing than talking. And, if you're like me and discover all too often that you've put your foot in your mouth, you may want to just keep dancing. It will remind you to do less talking and keep your feet where they belong.

Words that can heal

Be cautious about what you say, and be mindful of how your words may affect people. They can hurt or they can nurture. While many great philosophers could be cited here, I think of a cartoon character who said it just fine. Remember Thumper, in Walt Disney's *Bambi*? *If you don't have something nice to say, then don't say anything at all.*

In a medical setting, sometimes patients need to hear the truth. You can't talk a problem away. But watch out for people who repeatedly ask you for help or repeatedly complain about the same issue. They're the ones who continue to talk about why they can't lose weight or why they're still in a bad relationship or why they always have such bad luck. Those people are like energy vampires. I see them at the Clinic, I run into them socially, and I encounter them in relationships. They make the same mistakes over and over again, they have the same complaints about life, and they just want to talk, talk, *talk!*

I had a friend like this. One time she called just after I'd gone to bed. During the conversation I fell asleep and when I awakened, her voice was still jabbering from the receiver, which had fallen off the side of my pillow. Three hours had gone by and she was still talking! (Now I have caller ID. When the phone rings after bedtime, I don't answer it 95 percent of the time.)

With patients, I've found it necessary at times to interrupt the talking to point out some truths. If you do it lovingly, you can get away with saying things most people don't want to hear. And if a doctor can't be this courageous and tactful, who else can?

For example, one patient keeps complaining of the same pain. Over a period of five years, I've diagnosed him three different times. He keeps saying, "I can't make the appointment for the therapy you recommended. My marriage is still terrible, I still hate my job, and I'm in financial trouble again." Finally I looked him in the eye and told him, "You need to stop talking and start doing!"

I also have the courage to ask them about their spiritual faith, the activities that bring them solace, and the special people in their lives. This makes it easier to coax them into some form of counseling or psychotherapy eventually. Still, I have to be brave enough to accept their anger, denial, and noncompliance. To these patients, I say, "You're not ready to heal yourself. You're not ready to take control of your life. You're not ready to be accountable for your own well-being."

Many of the noncompliant patients I see have good insurance plans. Sadly, they're wasting this valuable resource, in my opinion. Meanwhile many, many patients who are uninsured and poor can only imagine what it would be like to go to a doctor's office for a chronic condition and just complain, much less be offered therapy!

It's a tricky dance when you're stepping between compassion and enabling. As a physician I must be acutely aware of this, since some patients can become so addicted to hearing words of compassion that they don't want to get better. They become afraid that if they do improve, I'll stop talking to them. I won't, of course, but a healer should not be an enabler.

Words of kindness and compassion also can influence healing through the placebo effect. Much research has been done to show that the patient's belief or trust in a healing procedure or drug may be as effective as the actual treatment. One such study involved a procedure in which a small bore hole was created in the skull in order to transplant nerve tissue in patients with Parkinson's Disease. Interestingly, several patients who received the placebo (the skull bore alone) but believed they had received the tissue implant progressed more favorably than some of their cohorts who had the full procedure. In fact, one of the patients who had received the placebo surgery discontinued medications during the one-year observation period.

Pleasing words are healing not only to those who hear them but also to those who pronounce them. In the book *How Full is Your Bucket? Positive Strategies for Work and Life*, authors Tom Rath and Donald O. Clifton distinguish between people who are bucket-fillers and those who are not. Bucket-fillers are those who share kind and generous words through sincere compliments, genuine encouragement, or support. Those who are not have no kind words for others. They may even deplete the contents of buckets, including their own. The authors cited a study of nuns who were followed for decades. The group of sisters who could have been described as bucket-fillers lived about ten years longer than the other nuns in the study. In fact, bucket-fillers had a better survival rate than people who quit smoking, who lived an average of seven more years. We health-care providers need to begin filling buckets by pushing preventive care, disease screenings, and patient education. Our patients will live longer, and so will we.

Unfortunately, it seems as if our culture is addicted to the wrong kind of talking.

Talking doesn't make problems go away

About the time I moved into my post-divorce dwelling – an old farmhouse, which was destined to be demolished – I began spending more and more time alone. As I avoided telephone conversations and stopped seeking fillers for the silence, I became aware of the sanctuary within myself.

I'm a tremendous social butterfly, but I've also learned to appreciate my own company and relish periods of solitude. In my modest little rental house, I found the great gift of silence and solitude. Being alone with myself has taught me to converse with myself and God. Ironically, once I learned this, I discovered that I had fewer problems than I thought, and I got more done. In this silence of deeper reflection, I could be more productive. I actually became a doer.

This reminds me of the philosophy of one of my dearest uncles, who is now deceased. An extremely effective and industrious businessman, Uncle Rene would say, "Jeannetty, there's no such thing as *problems*. This word is simply used to describe the challenges that people refuse to address or confront. A dilemma, a question, a project requires your immediate attention. I have no problems because I do not procrastinate over the solutions."

Words that can hurt

My ex-husband and I used to give sexual-harassment seminars at medical school. We were an ideal duo: the male lawyer, who was sympathetic to the female victim, and the woman doctor, who worked almost exclusively with men. One of the audience's take-home messages was that of basic etiquette. If you wouldn't say something provocative or controversial in front of your mother, wife, or daughter, why would you say it in the middle of a classroom, the corridors of a hospital, or in a surgical suite?

Some men describe women they encounter in professional settings and elsewhere as hypersensitive, yet these same men never give a thought to how their wives or daughters might be affected by the kind of demeaning environment such men are creating for others. It's also very presumptuous for these men to expect others who share their gender to enjoy this behavior. There are many good-hearted men who don't condone such actions.

I've always loved general surgery. It's the perfect marriage between art and science. Though I won honors during my surgical rotations at Case Western Reserve University and enthusiastic support from my chief resident and other professors, there were those who questioned whether a woman belonged in the harsh world of surgeons. During my later sub-internships in surgery, I encountered a different climate from that of the academic world. At several hospitals I was tested, not on anatomy, but on my tolerance for obscenity.

The culmination of such childishness took place when I was assisting in a surgical case and the patient was a very obese woman who had an inflammatory bowel disease. She was undergoing a bowel resection, which required a diversion of waste products through a stoma, which would empty from her abdominal surface into a bag. During the procedure I was asked for the umpteenth time a rude question about the consequences to male ejaculatory function of surgery in this area. After calmly answering the question, I asked the surgeon who stood across from my retractor, "What happens to female sexual function in this setting? After all, we're operating on a woman." "Goddamned feminist," he muttered under his breath, yet loudly enough for the other six men in the room to hear and chuckle over it. As luck would have it, every member of the surgical team, including the scrub nurse, was male.

The dissection of the bowel with its blood supply wasn't long enough to reach through the large layer of fat to the surface of the patient's skin. The surgeon became very frustrated and began calling her a "fucking pig." As his frustration grew and the expletives increased, he looked across the table at me, his eyes squinting, his forehead flushed. "Who cares about female orgasm anyway – they all fake it!" he hissed. I retorted, "We don't need to know about your personal experiences." The room was silent from that point forward, except for the exaggerated clattering of surgical instruments thrown, rather than placed, by a pouting middle-aged man.

A final word

I was asked during an interview what I thought was my greatest inspiration or asset. I replied without hesitation "My naiveté!" I've never allowed myself to be talked out of anything I wanted to do. And this is quite an accomplishment in light of the harsh and insulting discouragement I've endured.

By doing – by creating – you ignite inspiration. And while talking is sometimes necessary to analyze a situation or solicit support from others, it can also lead to discouragement if the wrong words are used. In fact, too much talking about something can often lead to people being *talked* out of doing things they really want to do.

Usually, when I'm dancing, I can't let myself get too involved in conversation, especially with leaders who are pessimists or complainers. Pessimists are easy to spot. They're the ones who try very hard to interrupt your dance with their should haves, could haves, and would haves. Phrases containing these words are big red flags!

When these folks are around, I exercise the only exception to my rule of "not rushing the dance." If you ever find yourself in this situation, dance fast and get away!

GLOSSARY

Tanda: A series of three to four tango dances separated by *cortinas* (short pieces of nontango music), which allow dancers to enjoy several dances in a row without interruption.

Chapter 11

Don't Dance as if 90 Percent of the Accountability Is Yours

As a novice dancer, I had a private tango lesson with the famous Diego di Falco, who starred in the Broadway hit *Forever Tango*. I was dancing as though it were entirely my responsibility, he told me. At first I was flattered (silly me). I thought I was showing him what an ambitious student I was. Later, I realized it was a criticism, a rather astute observation that not only applied to my dancing but held deep implications for my life.

Diego said that in the dance, I was putting too much emphasis on myself, I wasn't sharing the dance with him. I was thinking too much about how I could please the leader, how I would accomplish the moves, and how I would perform. Instead, I needed to concentrate on how we would perform together.

Here's one reason that this can be a problem. If you're so caught up in how you look or how you're going to perform, then you're already plotting your next move and how you'll respond to it. Thinking and anticipating so far ahead will affect your awareness of the present moment and may cause you to miss the leader's next cue or misinterpret the message he's giving you.

In addition, a follower who thinks that the dance is all about herself runs the risk of offending the leader. *Aren't I supposed to be calling the shots?* he may think and then decide that he never wants to dance with you again.

Someone who feels totally responsible for the dance is acting in a very controlling manner. Both partners are obliged to maintain the dance, and for that to happen, it's important that they always communicate, even if the "talking" is done through body language.

Dancing as if 90 percent of the accountability rests with you may at first seem like real ambition and dedication. But in truth, it's pure ego and self-obsession, which is the less-recognized female style of narcissism. Narcissism is an ugly word used in this case to describe a pretty woman who wants to assume responsibility for everyone else's well-being – even the fabulous man who leads like a dream and who is in very little need of rescue.

The pursuit of perfection

Women can have such a sense of responsibility and omnipotence. Whether in tango or elsewhere, we want to perform so well. We strive to be perfectionists in all respects. We manage our careers, households, and children while trying to fit what writer Betty Friedan called "the feminine mystique." This need to pursue perfection makes us enthusiastic dance students. We travel to workshops, study musicology, and practice in high-heeled shoes in spartan living rooms with invisible partners.

However, our industrious and productive qualities may actually hinder us. How can any woman obsessed with perfection allow her partner to lead?

Honestly, we women are our own worst critics. Being a superwoman or supermom feeds our egos, not our souls. Our quest to be so productive, energetic, pretty, and nice may seem on the surface so appropriate, so correct. But on the dance floor what seemed to work in the other world becomes nothing more than a glaring impediment. (It doesn't work too well in the real world either. Why else would so many women be taking Zoloft?)

Patient accountability

My patients have the responsibility to follow through on their therapies at home. Early in my career, I became extremely frustrated by those who did not heed my advice. For example, one patient continued to gain weight, requiring additional medications to control his rising blood pressure. Another wouldn't stop smoking and ignored his frequently recurring episodes of bronchitis. Another saw his back pain worsen after an injury because of his continued lack of exercise and rehabilitation.

Later I came to realize that getting angry at these patients was wrong. Anger is a demonstration of my ego, my effort to assume 90 percent accountability for the doctor-patient dance. I saw that I had to let my patients make their own choices regarding their health. Asking patients to adopt healthy habits or lifestyles without understanding the obstacles arising from their unique circumstances was not effective.

We physicians must understand what motivates our patients' manifestations of unhealthiness. Could it be that, deep down, they sabotage their own well-being because they don't feel worthy of happiness or health? Depression and anxiety disorders are extremely common and often lie beneath the surface of such physical complaints as obesity or hypertension. It's interesting to see how many people punish themselves by gaining weight or internalizing their anger (which often shows up as high blood pressure).

What I learned is that to get a true picture of how a patient relates to his health, I had to understand his sense of self-worth in the context of his life. I can't fix in one session someone who's been carrying around years of imbalance, but I *can* point out areas of life that are very full and rich. For some reason, this kind of validation is extremely powerful when it comes from a physician. It's such a wonderful gift to be able to inject optimism into a patient's prescription for self-care – yet I'm realistic enough to know that it's up to him to start his healthy regimen. As he begins to improve, it gets easier for him to continue living a healthier lifestyle because I can empower him through the success of what he has done. And with every success he experiences, I make it clear that *he* did it – he used his body's ability to heal itself. All I did was to provide guidance and compassion.

True compassion is wonderful. It's empowering and engaging, sincere and hopeful. It really helps people. Giving people anger and pity only serves to bury them deeper and deeper in a trench of self-loathing and despair, where rescue may not be possible.

Celebrating life

During my training, I delivered many babies and shed many tears of awe and joy in the process. I reveled in the privilege of participating in one of the most powerful events in nature. (And I mean *nature*, not medicine. People need to be reminded that pregnancy is a healthy, natural state of being, rather than a diagnosis.)

My "go-with-the-flow" style of birthing used to drive obstetrical nurses crazy. I trained in a rather conservative region of Ohio, where hospital staffers were just beginning to abandon the practice of administering enemas and shaving women's genitals in preparation for vaginal childbirth. So you can imagine how I was perceived when I allowed my patients to squat or push on all fours in a doggy position. Sometimes, women got so overheated during the transitional phase that they would strip completely. I wasn't affected by this, but some of the nurses were horrified. They were uncomfortable with women who were naked, noisy, messy, or earthy.

Additionally, the nurses were particularly perturbed by women who chose not to use pain relievers, especially epidurals. I noticed immediately that women who labored with the help of modern pharmacology were much less work: They were high-maintenance chicks with low-maintenance deliveries. I would walk into a delivery room and find the father watching television, the nurse in a corner documenting numbers from graphs monitoring the fetus, and Mom staring at her freshly painted toenails, wondering aloud when she should start using what she had learned in her Lamaze class. Call me unsympathetic, but I really disliked those sterile, artificial deliveries. What I enjoyed was passionate deliveries that engaged the medical staff and family members. With laboring mothers, I welcomed such human reactions as perspiration, tears, and moans, and encouraged caregivers to respond with backrubs, massages, and consoling words.

Nor did I forbid unusual positions. In one case, a patient suddenly rolled onto her side and was overcome with the urge to push. I performed a quick exam and found the baby descending appropriately. The nurse began to verbally and physically coax the patient back into a lithotomy position (on her back). My patient moaned, "I can't … please let me stay like this …"

While she was lying on her left side her contractions began, and she responded by raising her right knee. I lifted her leg and ducked underneath, placing her lower leg on my shoulder, and delivered her baby from this position. Hey, if the baby was doing fine, and Mom instinctively maneuvered into a position that worked better for her, I could easily follow her and reposition. After all, wasn't this supposed to be about her and not me?

I remembered a lecture given by a South African midwife. Behind their "modernized" birthing suites, which consisted of examining tables complete with stirrups, there were rooms with soft floors, pillows, and a thick knotted rope suspended from the ceiling. When native women were asked which room they favored, many grudgingly indicated the modern room. They believed they'd be inconveniencing the doctor if they didn't choose this Americanized style of birthing. "I want to make it easier for the doctor," was the response they most often gave. But if their midwife was attending their child's birth, women felt most comfortable standing, bending, or squatting as they hung onto the rope.

At another birth, which occurred during a very busy resident clinic, I was performing a six-week postpartum evaluation on a low-income patient, who was accompanied by her gorgeous chubby baby. As I stood admiring him she told me that she was breastfeeding him. Rarely did our patients breastfeed, and I, a La Leche League fanatic, was overjoyed to hear this. But the next moment, I was terribly disappointed to hear her express her desire to switch to bottle-feeding. I was tempted to write this case off as just another patient who preferred to use the baby formula subsidized by the WIC program. Instead I asked, "Why do you want to stop breastfeeding? You're doing a fabulous job – look how beautiful he is!"

She said timidly, "It makes me feel … like … an animal, Dr. Potts."

I smiled. While I performed some suggestive pelvic movements, I asked, "You've had sex? Yes?" She grinned. Then I squatted and, grunting, asked, "And you've given birth? Yes?" She began to giggle. "And … this?" I gestured to her chest. "Makes you feel like an animal?" We laughed so hard that we startled the baby.

At his one-year checkup, the mom was still breastfeeding, although her son had been eating table food since he was 6 months old. She was actually sad about the weaning process.

Self-indulgence

Lack of accountability in our society is certainly troublesome. But assuming all or most of the responsibility for others is equally troublesome. As a doctor, as a dancer, and as a woman, I must foster independence in others and allow my partners to fulfill their roles and to experience their destinies.

I know a fabulous dancer, Sherrie Pallotta, who is also a chef here in Cleveland. She told me once that guilt is a form of self-indulgence. Guilt and the need to please others impel women to dance as if we had 90 percent of the accountability. Her statement is a familiar expression of our own inflated self-importance.

When I focus on my missteps as I dance, it can be just as offensive to my leader as if I were boasting of my talent or accomplishments. Sometimes self-deprecation is just a way of fishing for compliments and getting more attention. It's a more subtle but also more pervasive form of narcissism.

In her book *The Labyrinth of Desire*, Rosemary Sullivan describes this characteristic after musing about Frida Kahlo's relationship to her husband, artist Diego Rivera:

> I am fascinated with female narcissism. We think of narcissism as self-love, but it is actually self-obsession. At its most extreme, it means being so trapped in a battle between self-hatred and self-love that the outside world ceases to exist except with reference to oneself. Every woman knows this battle, if only in a minor way. We are encouraged to fall in love with our own image, but then we can never be beautiful enough. Endlessly self-conscious, we assume the world is always watching and judging when, in fact, the world is indifferent to our small fates.

Keeping themselves under the microscope doesn't matter to people who are content with having fun as they dance. As the saying goes, "Dance as though no one was looking." People who believe this don't notice or care if the dancers around them are less than perfect. But those who do take notice of everyone else's imperfections – well, they're simply not dancing. Rather than experience life, they prefer to observe it.

Chapter 12

Learn to Dance, but
Let the Dance Teach You

I was 39 years old when I began dancing again, and I threw myself into my new rhythmic happiness with childlike abandon. I tripped the light fantastic in every form: salsa, meringue, swing, hip-hop. If I heard music, I moved to it. I danced in heels, flats, and bare feet. I wore jeans, Danskins, tight dresses, sultry gowns.

But I hadn't yet discovered tango, although I was familiar with the word. It conjured sensuous and dramatic images of tall, dark, and handsome men clad in tuxedos, who moved over the dance floor with seductive, catlike grace. The tango world seemed so exotic and unattainable.

One night, translators from Cleveland Clinic invited me to join them at the Peruvian Independence Day Ball. During the evening's entertainment, as the percussive music ceased, an announcer introduced three dancers who would perform an Argentine tango exhibition. But the partner of one of the men was absent, and the group asked for a volunteer. Friends at my table immediately volunteered me. I hesitated for about five seconds, then brazenly approached the dance floor.

The music began to play, but we didn't move. My partner transferred his weight from one foot to the other so gently, it felt as if he were taking a breath. I was certain that only I perceived his subtle motion. Then he began to lead me, but I didn't know how to follow. Yet deep down, something told me to trust him. He invited me to step in certain directions; he coaxed certain motions from my legs and feet. I perspired and became acutely aware of my awkwardness. The dance seemed painfully long.

When the music stopped, he escorted me off the dance floor like a gentleman. "How do I learn this dance?" I asked. He gave me his business card. His name was Rick Ramos. The card remained in a drawer for about six months before I made the decision to begin taking lessons with him in December 2001.

Under Rick's instruction, simple building blocks became elaborate dance steps. I was captivated by the nonverbal communication between man and woman on the dance floor, and I realized that the same approach could be applied to the rigors and stresses of daily life. Soon "dance" became the busiest verb in my vocabulary. I danced with my children, I danced with friends and co-workers, and I danced with my patients. Sometimes I led them; other times, I surrendered to their lead; and once in a while I playfully practiced interleading and "stole" the lead for a few movements. I began to appreciate my own axis, from which I derived courage and peace.

Beyond the erotic mystique, tango's fusion of physics, artistry, and passion provocatively illustrates the dialogue of our daily lives. Tango is spontaneous and unchoreographed. Two people can move as a fluid unit, which prevents costly and unnecessary errors. New meaning and strength are breathed into the ideas of cooperation, receptiveness, surrendering, and yielding.

After about six months of lessons, I had compiled quite a collection of thoughts and reflections connected with tango. The task of learning this dance opened new avenues of insight for me. Tango taught me about my shortcomings, insecurities, goals, and strengths, and it taught me as well about dialogue and relationships. And today, the dance continues to be my teacher. Tango holds me captive, and I am its perpetual pupil.

Many things to many people

When one of my medical school professors heard that I was coming out of the closet about my tango dancing, she was very concerned about the negative impact such a revelation might have on my medical career. One can only imagine her surprise at learning that I was taking my tango show on the road, presenting "Tango Lessons for Life" lectures at medical-society meetings – complete with a dance partner!

I was once confronted at a conference dinner party by the Uruguayan spouse of another invited lecturer. Rather arrogantly she declared, "An American woman would *never* be capable of dancing tango. She doesn't understand the culture or the history." I politely acknowledged the richness of her culture and its past, and went on to explain tango's universal appeal, which derives from its understanding of love and suffering. Despite the sometimes sordid and oppressive nature of tango's past, people could still experience the beautiful elements of surrender in the dance and incorporate such values into their daily lives. I realized that my appearance and lack of Argentine accent gave me no credibility in the woman's eyes when she quickly dismissed my comments.

I can honestly state that the neither the Argentines nor the Uruguayans hold a monopoly on tango dancing. I've danced with Argentine partners who were awesome and others who were dull. I've shared amazing dances with Russian, German, Japanese, Turkish, Italian, Spanish, Mexican, Dutch, Israeli, and American men. The common denominator among these wonderful leading men was the sense of yearning and reverence with which they shared their embrace. These men, it seemed, were far from their homes and families, and they cherished the solace derived from a woman's embrace and envelopment by melodies so rich with nostalgia.

During one of my New York City tango visits, I danced with a robust fellow from Turkey who made me feel like a precious flower. He held me closely and very softly. He paused at the most beautiful measures of the song and seemed to sigh. After the *tanda*, he escorted me back to my seat. I watched other dancers and felt pleasantly inebriated, sharing the room's collective embrace. Later I admired him as he danced with another *tanguera*. I felt privileged to witness the manner in which he savored the dance, and I delighted in recognizing his protective posture and the look of serene contentment on his partner's face. I thought, *This is how I looked, just moments ago, while dancing with someone who cherishes our beloved tango.*

Tango, like tango dancers, is often misunderstood. How can something so sensuous and provocative (at one time, it was even forbidden) be a source of spiritual inspiration and innocent pleasure? But tango is many things to many people. Those who know it intimately explore and define their interpretations differently. Although tango has form and technique, it is also free and interpretive. Paradoxically, it requires discipline in order for the dancers to achieve liberation. A French urologist and jazz aficionado I once met told me, "It is the profound knowledge of the rules and the structure that allow you to break free."

Being mindful

Find your tango, I tell people, *find your tango*. There must be something that you do that teaches you more about life and about yourself. It doesn't have to be something wild or exotic – maybe golfing or cooking is your thing. If that's the case, look at how you experience the putting green or the kitchen. Be aware of your feelings when you're in those environments, and try to adapt your insights to the dynamics of your workplace.

Whatever you do, do it thoughtfully. Perform your tasks mindfully. Anything you do mindfully, no matter how mundane that activity may seem at first, can become significant if it reminds you of the importance of your life. Around the time I began dancing again, I also created a series of drawings and poems titled "Love Songs and Prayers." This small project embodied my thankfulness for even the simplest daily activities. Among the love songs and sensuous drawings, there are prayers of thanksgiving for the gift of culinary arts, sleep and dreams, and water. In this series, water also symbolized the menstrual cycles, for "I, too, dance with the moon." I've come to recognize the beauty even in what so many women consider a curse.

Being mindful means paying attention. Being mindful means being aware of your attitude. In Rick Warren's *The Purpose Driven Life: What on Earth Am I Here For?*, the author reminds us of the dairymaid who, through her seemingly humble task, gives glory to God simply by being aware. A mindful person listens to himself and others. When you're doing that, when you just react to the moment, you're not composing an answer, analyzing, or interpreting. You're relaxed because nothing is expected of you except to listen, be aware, and pay attention.

The father of one of my high-school friends used to tell me that he offered up prayers as he worked in a factory in the morning and invented things in his lab in the afternoon. But in the evening, he'd quiet his mind and listen. "This is when God would give his responses," he said. I found this very endearing.

Being mindful can, at first, be scary because awareness is unfamiliar territory for most people. Being open to the moment involves giving up control. Unfortunately, we've been taught since we were youngsters that we should always *control ourselves*. Because if we weren't in control, we'd be less efficient, and before you know it, we'd see a decline in our productivity and career. We learned that we also need to control our emotions so that we don't divulge our true feelings and expose ourselves to the world.

I've come to realize that keeping myself under such tight control is a waste of personal energy. Staying in control requires so much energy. Fretting and worrying is a further waste of energy. Being aware of the moment puts your energy to better use.

Someone once asked me whether I'm still learning about dance. Absolutely. And one of the things I've learned recently is that I have even more to learn. Very advanced dancers, whom I admire, still take basic classes over again, just to ensure the integrity of the basic building blocks of tango.

We should't be afraid to revisit the basics from time to time. We may think we're beyond certain levels, but repeating an elementary lesson with mindfulness can be most enriching. It's like dancing with a beginner; appreciating a novice's struggles helps the advanced dancer reinforce his or her own fundamentals and learn even more. I suppose what I'm saying is that no lesson is beneath us.

When I conduct my workshops, some people tell me that they're not really interested in learning tango. But the point is that I'm not teaching tango – I'm using tango as a tool to spark awareness. So my questions to you are "What is your tango?" and "What does your bit of bliss do for you?" Whatever your answers, I hope that you're following a really great path. Just stay aware on your journey!

Always learning

I'm taught something new every day. I study journals and books, and analyze cause and effect in a dozen different ways. I continue to learn about the art of medicine through my patients. And many of my patients have become my teachers as they humbly shared their precious life experiences with me. Some have even spoken simple words that, unbeknownst to them, were filled with wisdom. They were truths I needed to hear in moments of need.

About ten years ago, I met a very tall, dignified, and soft-spoken 86-year-old man who was referred to me because he had blood in his urine.

I entered the room before he finished disrobing and noticed beneath the curtain that one of his legs was deformed.

The deformity of his right calf was so pronounced that I could scarcely believe that this was the same man who had walked so gracefully down the hallway moments earlier. After his exam, which was normal, I asked him about his leg. He hesitated for a moment, perhaps because he hadn't thought about his leg for some time.

"When I was 8 years old, I had a severe bone infection," he began. "The doctors wanted to cut the leg off. I went through many painful procedures to cut away the infection. For almost four years, they cut away so much of the skin and muscles." Indeed, this would have been the practice at that time. I could barely imagine a young boy enduring such tremendous pain and trauma in an era of far fewer pain remedies and no antibiotics.

"But you kept your leg," I said. "It's incredible."

"Yes, and it's because of my parents. They wouldn't allow the doctors to cut off my leg. And, Doctor, you can imagine how unusual it was, since I was a little black boy in the South and my parents were poor farmers. Some of the doctors thought my parents were crazy not to listen to them, but my mom and dad just took me to other doctors, even to other cities. I still don't know how they managed all the costs. But they found this doctor. He worked hard to save my leg." He pointed to the side of his calf, which I could now see had been made with a graft from a muscle taken from his thigh. "He did this surgery. But he said I'd never be able to really use it properly. He was saving the leg, but he didn't believe I'd ever really walk."

He gave a little chuckle. "Well, I could even run on this here leg and pretty fast, too. And I got a job and worked my whole life."

He stared into the distance for a moment before turning toward me again with a smile of quiet pride and accomplishment. That day I learned about humility, dignity, duty, and courage – all because I asked a quiet old man about his deformed leg.

Follow your truth

Confronting and surviving life's challenges in a joyful way requires a dance. I've known this for years. This dance of life may inevitably lead people to scuff their gorgeous shoes and injure delicate toes. Obviously, people preoccupied with the preciousness of their own toes and the luster of their own shoes will never learn to dance. But as Alan Kremen, M.D., Ph.D. (another tango afiocionado) observed, to learn the truths of love and life, you must experience the dance and allow yourself to be touched, moved, and embraced.

In *The Dancing Wu Li Masters*, author Gary Zukav writes that life is filled with awe and amazement, and it would be a pity to discard all the magical things that enrich our lives just because they can't be explained or understood in logical ways. "The dancers may claim to follow truth or claim to seek reality, but the Wu Li masters know better. They know that the true love of all dancers is dancing."

Psychologists also speak of the element of awe in our lives as a guide for our happiness and fulfillment. I believe that our religions and spiritual beliefs are the source of this awe, even if they can't be defined or explained in scientific terms. But as motivational speaker Bob Pritchard says, "The absence of evidence is not evidence of its absence."

Chapter 13

Recognize the Opportunity That Comes with Novelty

In August 2004, I was lecturing at an international prostate symposium in Santiago, Chile. Our hosts at the Hospital Aleman were lovely, and the gorgeous snow-capped Andes Mountains that skirted the city were breathtaking. As I was only a short jet flight away from Buenos Aires, I decided to take this fortuitous opportunity to visit my tango Mecca. Once there, I looked up a tango teacher named Mario, who had been highly recommended to me. At our meeting, he made the usual request for a first dance, to get a sense of my skill. I was used to this request, considering my many private lessons in New York City, Chicago, and Cleveland. I wasn't nervous about these *ad hoc* evaluations, since I had consistently and pleasantly surprised many Argentine instructors over the previous two years.

He proposed *"una Milonguita."* I must have looked extremely disappointed, judging from the look of alarm that developed on his face. I really dislike *milonga. Milonga* is a form of tango that is more like a mazurka or a polka. It's not very challenging. I find it boring, monotonous, and not at all sexy. (I had found only one person, until then, who could make the dance interesting – my teacher Timmy Tango.)

I began pouting, *"Pero no me gusta milonga."* ("I don't like *milonga.*")

His girlfriend/dance partner began to giggle. With his finger on the play button of his CD player, he pleaded with an innocent flirtatiousness. *"Por favor…"*

The music began. I sighed and grudgingly dragged myself to the center of the dance floor, thinking, "God! I'm in Buenos Aires and I'm going to begin my lessons with a *milonga?*"

Mario smiled mischievously and politely waited for me to initiate the embrace. I stood beside him – and within seconds I was transported into the marriage of music and movement. His lead was assertive and clear. We were syncopating, lunging, and embellishing coquettishly with our shoulders. He led me into high back kicks and pivots at varying and sometimes dizzying speeds. By the time the music stopped, my face felt frozen into one of the broadest smiles of my life. *Wow …*

"I told you so," he said with an impish wink.

The remainder of the ninety-minute lesson progressed with refinement of form and footwork as I was sumptuously lunged, dipped, and displaced to fabulous tango music. I even welcomed a couple more *milongas*. Eleonora, his partner in dance and life, observed our dances and commented, *"Tanta energia, hasta le salen por los deditos de sus pies."* ("So much energy, it even shows through her toes.")

Be open to change

With its quick, playful steps, *milonga* reminds me of a polka. It's a fast dance, with no languid movements or foot-dragging. Yet even though I'm a good polka dancer and actually I'm good at *milonga*, I just didn't find the dance sexy – until I danced it with Mario.

I allowed Mario to convince me to try just one *milonga*, and the experience blew me away. He made it fun and very sexy. I had no idea he did *milonga* with such intricacy. All it took was one dance with a master to change a prejudice that had been coloring my perception for years.

And then I realized something deeper within me. I didn't want to do *milonga* because I thought such a "boring" dance wouldn't test my dancing ability. I wanted to perform something that would make Mario's jaw drop in admiration. My ego had wanted to impress him with something more elaborate and dramatic.

All it took was one dance with a master to show me my bias. If I'd been more stubborn or he'd been a little less persistent, I might still be harboring this bit of dance prejudice today. I remind myself of this story as often as I can because there are probably a lot of other *milongas* around that I ignore or avoid wrongly.

Follow your heart

Nothing is more empowering than disproving someone's stereotype of you. For example, the other day the wife of one of my patients asked, "So how did a nice girl like you end up here?" As she said this, she gestured to the men in the lobby outside my office in the urology department, then glanced low and sideways toward her spouse's nether parts.

When I think about it, "What's a nice girl like you …?" has been the recurring theme of my life. Doctors and teachers, men and women, have tried to encourage me to pursue the medical disciplines for which they thought I was suitable. Others tried to humiliate me out of specializing in men's problems. But I refused to listen to anyone's stereotype of what a "nice girl-doctor" like me should do with her career. Instead, I followed my heart.

I remember my medical school rotations and the way I asked faculty members about the possibility of my pursuing urology as my career. As I told you earlier, I was so naïve that I wasn't in the least bit offended – in fact, I thanked them – for the way they practically laughed in my face, saying, "You're not gonna have any customers!"

So I interned in surgery and then completed subspecialty training in family medicine. One of my preceptors observed my unique background and wanted me to meet Dr. Andrew Novick, the chairman of Glickman Urological Institute at the Cleveland Clinic. At the time, I had no idea that he was internationally renowned in the area of urology, but I was flattered nonetheless by the introduction made by Dr. A.J. Cianflocco, from the orthopedics department.

Prior to our first meeting and the rigorous interview process that followed, I conducted my own little survey during rotations at the local Veterans Administration Hospital. As I was completing the physical examination of a patient who shared a room with three other men, I asked him, "Sir, if I were to become a urologist – you know, the kind of doctor who specializes in your prostate and your private parts – would you come to me for care?"

Without a second's hesitation, he nodded his head. "Why, of course I would!" But what was even more convincing was the response from the strangers on the other side of the curtain. Though they weren't even on our medical service, they chimed in almost in unison, "And I'd see you, too!"

I was honored that Dr. Novick, my chairman, offered me a fellowship that would prepare me for a position in the department as a medical urologist. I received my staff appointment one year later, in 1995.

My practice included diagnostic procedures and office-based surgery. Gradually, however, I rediscovered what originally impelled me to pursue a medical career and I saw what valuable tools I'd acquired through my family-practice training. I realized that men who suffered with chronic prostatitis or genital/pelvic pain were often misunderstood and too hastily treated with ineffectual conventional modalities. This evolved into a niche that has led to exciting collaborations, patient enthusiasm, controversial publications, and lectures as well as participation in international societies.

Now, over a decade later, as I look at my life in medicine, I see that I have indeed achieved my dream. And it happened despite the countless people who tried to talk me out of it without even getting to know me or seeing me in action, since they'd already made up their minds about what a female doctor in a male world could do.

And here's the funny thing. At first I believed them. But the Universe worked with me. Somehow my deepest desires became actualities. I learned surgery and became adept in family medicine, two disciplines that prepared me for a career in urology. I'm grateful to Dr. Novick, who saw beyond the stereotypes and did his own *milonga*.

In demand

In pursuit of a parallel job, I became involved with the activities of the *Confederacion Americana de Urologia* (the Latin American urological society) in the late 1990s and was appointed the society's director of education in 2000. My nickname among some of my Latino urological colleagues is *Chispa* (spark). These "brothers" of mine have brought much joy and laughter into my life. And more important, in the Latin American milieu I've been respected and celebrated as a knowledgeable professional as well as a spicy Latina.

Among some of my frequent invitations in South America are double requests to lecture at the scientific meeting during the day and to sing at formal events in the evening. In Venezuela several of us were given a rehearsal studio and in Brazil I sang with a band. Once it was *a capella*. And I've certainly performed dances. The most memorable of these was an impromptu flamenco performed with the former president of CAU and my beloved friend, Dr. Paul Escovar.

On that occasion, a group of professional dancers accompanied by live musicians had just cleared the floor after delighting the crowd of 600 urologists and their spouses. Paul rose from his seat of honor, scanned the audience, and *bam!* His look was unmistakable and his outstretched arm guided all eyes to the target. I rose, wove my way between the seats, and extended my own hand in response to his dramatic summons to the dance.

The guitarist began some earthy gypsy riffs. I adopted Paul's theatrics easily and proceeded to strike the flamenco posture, lifting my arms as my fingertips caressed the air. Our dance was beautiful, if I do say so myself. Paul's wife thought so, too, and even years later has suggested that for my consulting business I perform flamenco in addition to tango. While I do appreciate her compliment, I'm unable to give this other art form the dedication it deserves.

At one time Pfizer repeatedly asked me to present educational/promotional lectures on Viagra. The company appreciated my unique perspective as a female doctor for men. However, I wasn't prepared to call myself an expert on sexual medicine.

At the same time, something needed to be said. After all, the number of women in medical school is growing; recent statistics say medical school populations are now 50 percent or more female. So I thought it was important to share my insights and experiences, and to reassure and empower other female physicians about their role as caregivers to men.

The research I conducted while composing my lecture corroborated my feelings and years of experience. Women are excellent communicators; we're far less threatening than men; and our nurturing character gives us a unique vantage from which we can more readily diagnose and treat multifactorial maladies – that is, sicknesses that may arise from physical, emotional, and psychological changes. In terms of getting an overall idea about the health issues of male patients, it's very important to ask them about their sex lives. This question opens a window on the status of a patient's cardiovascular health, self-esteem, career satisfaction, psychological well-being, and relationships.

The theme of these lectures was "What's a nice girl like you …" During one of my lectures, which I conducted in a fabulous restaurant with a cooking studio, I also demonstrated one of my favorite Mexican recipes. The title of my lecture was a bit lengthy, but it was delicious: "Abolishing Myths: Nice girls can talk about sex, *and* Mexican cooking can be haute cuisine!"

Chapter 14

Be Glad Your Glass Is Half Empty

In terms of possessions, sometimes not having everything is good. The more you own, the more you have to juggle your time, family obligations, and bills (not to mention your sanity); the more you have up in the air at the same time, the greater the possibility that you'll drop something.

Don't get me wrong. I like having a nice home to live in, a reliable car, and the opportunity to provide for my children's needs. But when it comes to extra possessions, when I'm debt-free and carrying less of a load I feel lighter and am much more agile as I move through life.

Similarly, when I have few emotional worries, I'm lighter on my feet and freer to be in the moment. I'm a better dancer; I have a strong axis and can do all sorts of moves.

And I take risks because I don't have to worry about my balance. It's perfectly fine.

This is how I interpret that old saw about the glass being half empty. When it's half full, you might be expecting to fill it more. But do you really need a full glass? Do you *really* need that much water? And if you think you do, how will you pay for it?

Debt brings so many people down. Debt is the norm in this country; Americans are accustomed to it. There's such a high expectation surrounding our standard of living, and we define it in such a materialistic sense. All too frequently, debt appears to be the result.

Europeans live more simply, but they enjoy life more. My friends in Europe look at how we live and tell me, "I don't need all that stuff. I don't need all those gadgets." When people feel burdened by debt, they feel so limited. But they don't recognize that their debt is self-imposed. They are, unfortunately, obsessed with filling their cups all the way.

I practice what I preach. One of my goals in life is to avoid debt. With me, it borders on obsession. But this approach gives me such freedom. I have no worries. I'm not attached to anything. So I'm glad my glass is half full.

I'll tell you a story. My house is an entire dance floor, complete with an obstacle course. One day, my son was feeling a little sad. He was anxious about his school course load, and family matters were upsetting him. He became more quiet than usual and seemed preoccupied. Though he's a young man of few words, he's concise when he wishes to express himself. (I admire this quality in him very much.)

At the time, he was only 10 years old. He told me that he felt as if too many things were going wrong. I asked him to look at all the good in his life and brought him to realize that while yes, bad things happen to us, goodness is always present.

"It's like that phrase about the glass being either half empty or half full," I told him. "You know, honey, I think I've discovered a secret. Everyone's glass has exactly the same amount of liquid. It's half-filled. And you know what else? Some people think their glasses are bigger than everyone else's, and others see only an empty glass. So the secret in life is to realize that half a glass is perfect. Know why?"

He thought for a moment, then waited for my answer.

"Because, if the glass were full, we'd spill water every time we danced!"

The empty cup

Recognizing that your cup is half empty is a good way to enjoy and appreciate your life. Gary Zukav has a story in his book *The Dancing Wu Li Masters* that takes this idea one step further.

A Buddhist monk received a pilgrim who was seeking the secret of enlightenment. The monk gave a sage nod, then poured tea into their cups so the tea overflowed. The startled pilgrim asked the monk why he hadn't stopped pouring. The monk smiled and pointed out that the young man needed to come with an empty cup, because he could not learn if he came to the temple carrying a burden of preconceptions, prejudice, and judgments. So the pilgrim had to start his journey toward enlightenment with an empty cup – the "beginner's mind," as some Buddhists call it.

In a sense, my learning tango was like starting over with an empty cup. I began with a lot of preconceived notions. I thought that tango was all about technique, that learning to tango meant learning a series of steps, just as I might memorize a series of words in order to speak a foreign language.

Then I learned that I had a lot to unlearn. I had to discard what I'd picked up from other types of dances. I also had to learn humility. Until tango came along, I thought that dancing was all there was to dance – if you could twist, if you could polka, you could tango.

Wrong. I had to start with an empty cup. In doing so, I came to realize that you don't learn a dance; the dance teaches you.

Now I'm not knocking anyone who approaches dance with a different agenda. ("I'm dancing because I'm going to pick up chicks," "I don't care about all these moves out on the floor, I'm dancing because this is great exercise.") There are a million reasons to have an empty cup. But it takes a true student to fill that cup mindfully.

Another way of looking at the empty cup is seeing it as being in a pure state. The emptiness is clean. There are no preconceived notions about how the cup will fill itself. Simply, the cup exists to be filled.

For example, if you're taking a lot of preconceptions into a new job, relationship, or any other situation, the experience will be defined by your expectations – expectations that the other person or situation may not be able to live up to. But if you're empty in the sense of having no expectations, then you can be open to any possibility. And who knows? Perhaps what happens at your new job or the friendship that grows out of your new acquaintance will be even better than anything you ever could have imagined.

As a young girl I began plugging my ears when people would say things like "just you wait until …" I continue to plug my ears to this day. Consequently, I'm still a liberal, I still like men, I love surgery – and I even like teenagers!

(Remember the first rule of tango? *Do not anticipate!*)

What are you holding onto?
If your cup overflows, it may be time for you to examine what you're keeping in that cup. Those contents may not

be significant. You may be mixing together job projects, family obligations, career expectations, financial planning and wealth accumulation, and a network of relationships – and all those things might not fit in your cup.

Then, when it overflows, that's the signal of bad prioritization. When the cup starts overflowing, it's our responsibility to see how our self-indulgence is causing that overflow.

Your personal and family relationships are by far your greatest priorities, and they're what should fill your cup. Healthy relationships should never make your cup overflow.

Being glad that your house is half empty is just another spin on having a good outlook. It has to do with simplicity and lack of waste, and that old saying, "Be careful what you wish for." Sometimes enough is enough. And the half-glass is just enough.

A wise man once said, "When we come to the end of our life, it's not the things we did that we regret, it's the things we never did." Sometimes we never get to do the things we really would or should want to do; there's no more room in our cups. Our cups may already be fuller than we realize!

Chapter 15

Trade Places:
Ladies Learn to Lead,
Gentlemen Learn to Follow

Leading is an art form that melds physics and engineering to create fluid movements – the aesthetics of the dance. Following is also an art form, but it has its own special aspects requiring balance, strength, and agility.

When following, a dancer uses her body as a paint brush. With the music serving as inspiration, the couple paints a masterpiece. The leader relies on physics; torque, and leverage as he uses centrifugal force to put the follower into motion. So dancing isn't just about his leading a step. In addition, his partner is going to move according to the impulse and momentum he conveys.

A wonderful thing happens with the *molinete*. The man is leading, but it's up to the woman to carry that step. If he's only pivoting in the center as an axis, he's not going to get enough turn and the resulting flow won't be as beautiful, for she won't be able to move all the way around the circle. To complete the move, the follower has to throw herself back and create momentum, much as a tetherball winds itself around the pole. That's simple physics. If she leans back, she creates an acceleration momentum. If she's too stiff, the couple may only go halfway around. Not a pretty sight.

Even though so much of the dance is improvised, the leader must choreograph in his mind and think one step ahead. He does this while navigating a crowded dance floor and staying aware of his partner's footing and balance, which protects her from injury that might arise from contact with him or other dancers.

He glides, yet sinks his weight into the floor. Dancing with his heart, he remains in front of his partner, and she does the same with him. Further, he leads with his chest, even if he's not in physical contact with his partner's chest. His arms and shoulders do not orchestrate pivots and turns; instead, his entire torso steers her as he twists from his hips. The positions he desires to move into are communicated from his gut.

Like syncopations and slow or quick strides, the follower perceives a "gathering" of energy from the leader, an anticipation on his part that's a cue for something expected. The gathering of this energy and intention is perceived as a deep inbreath, a pause, or a rising of the body. Then comes the change in speed, the double step, or any number of embellishments meant to surprise and delight.

Out of respect, the leader acknowledges that his partner isn't a mind reader. His distinct yet subtle message is an invitation to join him and share each precious moment of a beautiful song. A good leader seeks to share his playtime in the most sincere fashion, composing, orchestrating, and trouble-shooting as he proceeds.

Upon realizing his discipline and appreciating his sensibilities, could any *tanguera* take a good lead for granted? Impossible! And if she were to try leading herself, her reverence towards a good *tanguero* would be immeasurable. That is, if a woman tries to learn the lead, she soon realizes how challenging it is, thereby kindling her admiration and respect for her dance partners.

The inadequate leader

The inadequate tango leader may feel threatened as his once meek and apologetic follower learns his weaknesses – weak techniques, hesitant maneuvers, and the quick hiss of an insult whispered in her ear. She remembers other leaders, who, like herself, are motivated and disciplined. She considers teasing him with an interlead or even stealing the lead. If she did that, would he feel threatened?

Ironically, the most macho leading men are the ones who would discourage this untraditional pursuit. They look upon her as disrespectful, brazen, and perhaps even immoral. How dare she tamper with the balance of power? How dare intelligent, talented women invade territory historically assigned to men?

Strong leaders who appreciate strong women are rare. Strong men aren't intimidated by women who take risks, make mistakes, and learn to overcome and persevere. The admiration such men display is based on respect and empathy – not neediness.

Mediocre tango leads and insecure leaders tend to seek out beginners. It's easier for them to win compliments and admiration from novices. On the other hand, there are many wonderful *tangueros* who ask beginners to dance from motives of good will and generosity, wishing to initiate novices further into this great pastime. How do you tell the difference? Mediocre and insecure leaders want to rule, not to share and teach. And under an inadequate leader, the dance becomes a power struggle.

Here's another mark of an insecure leader: jealousy. A good teacher is proud to see his pupil excel and even surpass the teacher. An inadequate leader is disappointed to see the follower equal his accomplishments. He feels the threat of the partner who wants to take over that lead – even if it's just for a little while. It's too bad these people become jealous and won't celebrate their partners' accomplishments or successes. How sad that there are people who will, when you surpass them, try to betray you.

The greater the leader, the more aware he is of his challenges. So to lead beyond one's ability is deceptive. Watch out for leaders who delegate without taking the time to understand the obstacles or the challenges you have to go through to complete a task. Pressuring people to perform and not telling them what's really required of them or where they could go for assistance is a very insensitive way to lead.

Grabbing the lead

A good leader will not start a new move or a new sequence until the follower has both finished and regained her axis. He takes responsibility for the dance. He adds a touch of playfulness to the movements. And he's not intimidated by a woman who moves with authority or steals the lead gracefully.

This is also how it is in the working world, where things are not yet as they should be. We still have a long way to go before women are perceived naturally in roles of leadership or roles of great strength and power. There still is that back step when people see a woman in a position of power. We really have a long way to go.

But things are changing for followers. Let me give you an example. I was doing a leadership workshop at the annual meeting of the fifty-seven mayors of northeast Ohio cities and before my presentation, one of the mayors started talking about his staff. He acknowledged all the hard work that his staff has done and joked, "You know, they don't even listen to me. It's like I'm not even there; they just do all this great stuff."

This gave me a great segue into my presentation. I was about to discuss the *molinete* and the power of the leader, and the follower's power in taking that lead and making it look good. And here was a mayor who trusted people – empowered people – enough to joke publicly about it.

He has a productive administration that works well with him. His staffers support him as much as he supports them. I'll bet his community is thriving.

Changing attitudes

Sometimes, all you need to burst the bubble of a stereotype is to be in the right place at the right time. Let me tell you another story of how I had my eyes opened – and how I was able to open some eyes around me.

Remember when I told you I was studying the mummies in Guanajuato, Mexico? I left Mexico in 1985 and began planning for medical school. For a time I took a job selling automotive parts and then heavy-duty equipment in Latin America. I was an importer and exporter for a small distributor in Cleveland, specializing in heavy-duty trucking and industrial equipment. I was familiar with parts from Detroit Diesel Allison, Bendix, Cummins Engines, and some offshore makers of crankshafts and other motor parts.

At first I thought I couldn't do this "masculine" kind of work because my male customers expected me to know more about crankshafts and transmissions than the other salespeople did. After studying several manuals, though, I realized that in fact I did know more than they did. But my smugness disappeared when, while entertaining my clients, I found myself in the most famous and controversial whorehouse in Mexico.

The night was young when a group of us decided to go out on the town after attending the reception at an annual trucking-parts convention. This very large international convention took place in Guadalajara, Jalisco. A Jamaican fellow hailed the cab and five of us got into the car. I asked the driver where we were going. "Do not worry, miss, it is *familiar*." He said this with a wink in his voice, as if we were going to visit family.

We arrived at a sad-looking three-story building with few windows, which intermittently brightened with flashes from pulsing strobes or purple beams of light. At the entrance we were all examined with a metal-detecting wand and lightly frisked. I wasn't suspicious about this, since I had been to nightclubs in Mexico City where entrances were lined with lockers in which guests could store their guns until they left the premises.

Each floor of this building offered a different type of music. *Ranchera/norteno* music was on one floor, rock and heavy metal played on another, and disco music thumped on the top story. We entered an extremely large room with traditional *norteno* music and cement floors. Drunken men crowded the room, and their loud, coarse voices drowned out everything but the thumping bass pounding from a crude string of speakers. I squeezed between the perspiring bodies of chain-smoking men, cursing that cab driver under my breath. I noticed a few women, standing – or were they posing? – between groups of very unattractive men. With a start, I suddenly realized that I was the only woman in the room with her clothes on.

The women were expressionless. Dyed blond hair could not conceal their indigenous heritage as they stood like olive-skinned mannequins, their exotic but lifeless eyes oblivious to the increasing drone of brutality. Some of them gazed down upon the crowd like rocks on a shoreline, indifferent to the rising violence of a stormy surf.

I was surprised to find myself looking right into the eyes of these women, completely unabashed. I was conducting business and so were they. Their clients – some of whom were *my* customers – were dreadful, and these women were literally risking their lives. Why did they pursue this line of work? To feed a child – or a drug addiction?

My compassion toward these women surprised me. How sorry I felt for their plight. I noticed the shabby, poorly hung curtains that covered a series of cubicles on the other side of the room. Was there a bed or even a chair within? How much did it cost to take a woman into one of those darkened stalls? What if I just gathered these women up, paid their pimp, and gave them a night of dignity?

But what is dignity? And who was I to judge?

The roaring of the sea of men grew louder. A woman poised herself on a small round platform and began undulating to the pulse-pounding music. Her long black hair rippled off the sides of her face like little stairs. She thrust her pelvis seductively, and some of the men began howling like blood-thirsty wolves.

My blood turned to ice. I had to get away before the wolves began feasting. I took leave of my clients and wove my way toward the door past several naked women and far too many caricatures of men.

The following morning, I sat eating alone as I came to terms with the end of my career in international business. My boss had never imagined placing a woman in my position before, and now, just after I had won his confidence, I'd have to explain my major shortcomings: I was unable to consume large quantities of alcohol or be entertained by naked women performing sex acts that were somehow intended to make men feel good about themselves. (I admit that I was stereotyping at that moment and not considering the many fine men in international sales who were *not* alcoholics or sexual degenerates.)

As I ate my breakfast, one of my clients came to my table to express his appreciation of me. Another came over to praise my companionship and apologize for the destination. Yet another told me how impressed he was by my professionalism. "You didn't embarrass us or embarrass yourself," he said. "We shouldn't have been there, and you handled it gracefully." The last one approached as I paid my check. "You are indeed a lady," he said. "Will you ever forgive us?"

I didn't have that disappointing talk with my boss after all. And my clients never seemed disappointed after that about conducting business with a lady – at, uh, less *familiar* places. But just when I was getting the hang of international business, I was accepted to medical school. I actually believed that I'd be leaving sexism and vulgarity behind me.

New roles

A few years ago, one of my beloved colleagues was inspired to propose a new role for me. He had just served as a guest lecturer at UCLA, where he had heard about the Berman sisters, who are specialists in female sexuality. He was impressed by their public personas and appeal to the media and thought that I could be their Midwestern counterpart.

I was paged to come to the chairman's office, where two very enthusiastic men made me a very attractive proposition. I was certainly taken by surprise and I genuinely appreciated their intentions. Indeed, I felt honored, especially considering the source of the proposal.

After I expressed my appreciation, I explained that I couldn't give up my male urological practice.

They were shocked. Until that moment, I don't think anyone, including me, knew how much I loved taking care of men. I knew that if I expanded my specialty, I'd see fewer patients, perform fewer vasectomies and biopsies, and treat fewer prostate problems. I'd miss the interactions that inspired the open dialogue that my patients and I enjoy.

Men have frequently expressed their appreciation for the unique sanctuary I've given them. They've described a comfort level they hadn't experienced with male physicians. Indeed, we address many issues pertaining to relationships and intimacy. I find this aspect of my practice very rewarding.

So with gratitude I declined this alluring proposition and stood up to leave. As I reached for the doorknob, I paused a moment and then said, "I do believe I accomplish more for female sexuality by taking care of men."

Further challenges

As I continue to practice to be a leader, I become more aware of the challenges of the dance. It's difficult to maneuver people who aren't light on their feet. Leading a pivot when the follower has no axis of her own is nearly impossible. This has been quite a learning experience. Wishing to be light and agile, I work harder now to strengthen my own balance and axis.

Also, having experienced the sabotage of my lead through a follower's anticipation has further burnished my readiness skills. My improving axis has led to a broader repertoire of possibilities, especially since I can now visualize maneuvers more clearly from the man's perspective. Just as in life, an unbalanced, clinging woman can make for a tiresome, boring dance.

By learning more about the tango lead, I've grown to appreciate my partners even more. I've become (I hope) a more sensitive follower. And, unexpectedly, I've also grown to appreciate myself.

I wish some men could feel the sensation of being a follower and know what it's like to walk backward and trust the impulse. Or feel the precariousness of high-heeled shoes combined with the exhilaration of high, sensuous *sacadas*. Or make turns that lift the skirt and send one's hair swinging.

Women can step into trousers and men's low-heeled tango shoes. Unfortunately, it isn't possible for men to switch into our shoes and costumes. But I still wish men could do more than simply lead. Because they don't practice following, they really don't know what they're missing.

I love being a *tanguera*!

Chapter 16

Surrender

In English, "surrender" has several connotations, many of which imply loss or weakness.

But in Spanish the word for surrender is *entregarse*, which comes from the verb "to deliver." Unlike the depressing feelings conjured up by the English word, *entregarse* has no negative connotations. Indeed, it's a beautiful and sensuous word, and one of my favorite words in Spanish. It implies a deliverance of oneself to a person – especially a lover, a cause, or a purpose – with complete abandonment of the self. In English the distinction may be made clearer by the qualifier "sweet," as in "sweet surrender."

Surrender isn't resignation, it's an acceptance. The ideas of surrender and acceptance give people a lot of peace, especially people who endure certain hardships. And we learn from the generosity of their stories that instead of suffering from indecisiveness or complaining in self-pity, we can put our troubles aside and move on.

As a follower, I surrender to my partner. When I'm being led into a precarious dip and allow my hair to sweep the floor, I don't perceive myself as weak. However, I notice that some people appear to become squeamish when I speak about the dance in such a manner. It's as though I've spoken explicitly about sex. Passion, surrender, abandon, sensuality! Can't these words of love also exist in our work, our food, our friendships, and our dance? Ironically, it seems from what thousands of men have shared with me that such surrender isn't taking place even in their marital beds.

In certain situations, surrender is the right course. When you're brave and strong, you surrender to the situation. Just as, in turn, the partner surrenders to his lead.

Detachment and trust

The concept of surrender has made me realize that one can't cling to anything or anyone. I can't possess the things I treasure most.

Buddhism clearly demonstrates this with the practice of detachment. According to that mode of thought, emotional investment in things or events outside ourselves creates expectations and feelings of self-importance within us. Think about it. Why are we trying to keep up with the Joneses? Is it really important or even meaningful to us if the neighbors have a better car? If we have no control over their choices, is it smart to let those choices affect us?

We can decide to take a different attitude and stop giving priority to things outside ourselves that are beyond our control. That's the beginning of the practice of detachment. Over time, our humility deepens as our sense of self-importance fades, and as we take our focus off things outside us, our insights start coming from within, where we experience wisdom and tranquility.

In *The Power of Now*, Eckhart Tolle talks about the choices we make in our lives. We can choose to remain trapped by a situation, complaining and perpetuating our feelings of helplessness. Or we can choose to be in the "now" moment, when we must assume accountability for our actions and initiate action to cause change. The third choice is to choose to remain, which implies an acceptance of the situation – in other words, a surrender.

Tolle believes that when your mind is completely quiet and you're purely experiencing the moment, that's a form of surrender. You're not constantly rethinking the past or anticipating and worrying about the future. You're not riddled with fear or displaying uneasiness and insecurity. Instead, you're in the "now" moment, trusting the Universe. You're so trusting, in fact, that you have no need to try to control a situation. You trust in the process, and your surrender is really a sign of faith.

In *The Purpose Driven Life*, author Rick Warren is critical of the emphasis many people place on fulfillment in the here and now. Instead, he focuses on eternity as a means of deriving peace and purpose. While I agree with him, I also bear in mind that too much of a focus on eternity or the hereafter can distract many people from their accountability now, their purpose and duty now, and the beauty that exists even during adversity, now! How can people appreciate and revere eternity if they can't grasp the sacredness of the here and now? After all, isn't eternity an infinite number of "now" moments?

Was Jesus a tango dancer?

When you follow, you sense yourself being cradled. You feel cherished in a man's arms. His heartbeat is strong and his breathing matches yours, right down to the pauses between breaths, which mirror the musical measures. He adjusts to your height, embraces you entirely, inhales your scent, and holds you even closer. He listens with his soul and moves according to your capability. He leads so well, you forget that your skill may not match his.

You're not afraid to press your entire ventrum against him and you're unafraid of letting go. When he entices you to lean back, you allow your hair to sweep the floor. He may seem slight, but he's exceedingly strong. You never fear falling because he would never allow this to occur. He'd never injure, harm, or embarrass you. He's proud to have you as his partner.

He navigates the dance floor. You have no idea where he's taking you, but he's worthy of your trust. So trustworthy, even, that you're tempted to give in to the moment and close your eyes.

Go ahead, try it. Learn to enjoy dancing with your eyes closed.

This is surrender. This is faith. This is what it would be like if we could dance with Jesus or Siddhartha or Ba'Hai. (Perhaps we can dance with them in spirit by trying to be like them off the dance floor and make this world a better place.)

Faith in the dance is also faith in the process of living. And more important, it's faith in yourself.

In the runic tradition, runestone number 13 is *Jera* – "Harvest." *Jera* is the stone that symbolizes the encouragement of success based on staying mindful in your work. In other words, you really can't push things; life reveals itself one day at a time. The parable associated with *Jera* is that of the farmer who was so eager to see his crops grow that he went out at night and pulled on the sprouts. Naturally, the plants grew irritated with the farmer and grew even more slowly. The moral of the story: Let things grow in their own time. Surrender to the process.

Surrender can also be a process of discovery. By this I mean that we can grow spiritually by exposing ourselves to the experience of surrender at different levels. Yes, it may feel as if we're taking some risks, and they may include making a commitment to learning something new – especially if they expose a lack of knowledge or athleticism, or something that you'd rather keep concealed. Sometimes the risk is more intimate, as in situations where you're surrendering not only to a process, but also to an individual to whom you feel vulnerable economically, emotionally, intellectually, or spiritually.

But eventually, the process of surrender leads you to a point where your risks become more intuitive than calculated. This is where you begin to realize that what's involved may not so much be trust in an individual or a situation. As in the dance, I began to realize that my growing comfort and trust were actually derived from my own self-awareness rather than the trust I felt in the ability of my dance partner. I realized that I could easily extinguish my need to anticipate and instead surrender the lead, even when dancing with strangers. It was a spiritual epiphany to recognize that I was surrendering only to myself, to my very essence, my soul – and because my soul has God, I believe I have become more capable of surrendering to my faith.

This reminds me of medical school and residency training. Those of us who were continually able to practice our surgical skills greatly appreciated the trust with which we were rewarded. But when we mused about the qualities of our teachers, it always seemed that among our professors, the ones who were the most talented and confident were also the ones who gave their junior colleagues or students the most opportunities to perform. So it wasn't entirely about our talents and trustworthiness. Our professors also possessed a self-awareness that allowed them to empower others through quiet, unpretentious supervision. A surgical chairman once told his residents, "There's no surgical error from which I can't rescue you …" Wow – how fabulously empowering!

So, as a final note – or perhaps I should say for the last step of this dance – learn to trust. Trust in yourself and begin to trust in your own intuition. Recognize that you're developing inner strength. Become aware of the surrender to self. And if you believe that your soul also has a piece of God within it, then surrender to God. Surrendering isn't a form of weakness or defeat; it's a manifestation of faith and strength.

Dance with as many people and situations as you can. Those couples who dance exclusively with each other grow to anticipate one another's steps and reactions. In other words, they may look like fabulous dancers, but are they *genuine* dancers?

A real leader can make another dancer – even a stranger – look fabulous. A real *tanguera* can follow any lead. So, like a fine tango dancer, don't anticipate. Instead, open your heart. Get to know people of different cultures and religions. Strengthen your axis by fortifying your heart and broadening the frontier of your experience. Test your axis by accepting challenges to your faith and equilibrium.

Believe you have the qualities to be a trusting, loving human being and a great dancer. Realize that heaven can be contained within each embrace.

Thank you for this dance.

Index

Other Books from Cleveland Clinic Press

Age Well! A Cleveland Clinic Guide

Arthritis: A Cleveland Clinic Guide

Autopsy – Learning from the Dead: A Cleveland Clinic Guide

Battling the Beast Within: Success in Living with Adversity
(about multiple sclerosis)

Breastless in the City: A Young Woman's Story of Love, Loss,
and Breast Cancer

Forever Home
(a chapter book about homelessness and loss for young readers)

Getting a Good Night's Sleep: A Cleveland Clinic Guide

The Granny-Nanny: A Guide for Parents and Grandparents
Who Share Child Care

Heart Attack: A Cleveland Clinic Guide

Heroes with a Thousand Faces: True Stories of People with
Facial Deformities and their Quest for Acceptance

One Stroke, Two Survivors:
The Incredible Journey of Berenice and Herb Kleiman

Lessons Learned: Stroke Recovery
From a Caregiver's Perspective

My Grampy Can't Walk
(multiple sclerosis from a child's perspective)

Overcoming Infertility: A Cleveland Clinic Guide

Planting the Roses: A Cancer Survivor's Story
(about esophageal cancer)

Sober Celebrations: Lively Entertaining Without the Spirits
(alcohol-free entertaining)

Stop Smoking Now! The Rewarding Journey to a Smoke-Free
Life – A Cleveland Clinic Guide

Thyroid Disorders: A Cleveland Clinic Guide

To Act As A Unit: The Story of the Cleveland Clinic
(Fourth Edition)

Women's Health: Your Body, Your Hormones, Your Choices –
A Cleveland Clinic Guide

Write for Life: Healing Body, Mind, and Spirit
Through Journal Writing

Cleveland Clinic Press

Cleveland Clinic Press publishes nonfiction trade books for the medical, health, nutrition, cookbook, and children's markets. It is the mission of the Press to increase the health literacy of the American public and to dispel myths and misinformation about medicine, health care, and treatment. Our authors include leading authorities from Cleveland Clinic as well as a diverse list of experts drawn from medical and health institutions whose research and treatment breakthroughs have helped countless people.

Each Cleveland Clinic Guide provides the health-care consumer with practical and authoritative information. Every book is reviewed for accuracy and timeliness by Cleveland Clinic experts.

For more information, visit www.clevelandclinicpress.org.

Cleveland Clinic

Cleveland Clinic, located in Cleveland, Ohio, is a not-for-profit multispecialty academic medical center that integrates clinical and hospital care with research and education. Cleveland Clinic was founded in 1921 by four renowned physicians with a vision of providing outstanding patient care based upon the principles of cooperation, compassion, and innovation. *U.S. News & World Report* consistently names Cleveland Clinic as one of the nation's best hospitals in its annual "America's Best Hospitals" survey. Approximately 1,500 full-time salaried physicians at Cleveland Clinic and Cleveland Clinic Florida represent more than 120 medical specialties and subspecialties. In 2006, patients came for treatment from every state and 100 countries. For more information, contact www.clevelandclinic.org.